Oil & Vinegar

D0127838

Vinegar	Page	Homemade	For Salads	For Fruits	For Marinating & Preserving	For Drizzling on	For Sauces	For Chutneys	Used on Pages
Apple Vinegar	12		●	●	●			●	42, 58, 59, 60
Balsamic Vinegar	6		●	●	●	●	●		7, 40, 48, 52
Bay Leaf Vinegar	14		●		●		●		44
Beer Vinegar	15		●				●	●	60
Blossom Vinegar	17	●	●	●	●				10, 58
Garlic Vinegar	16	●	●		●			●	44
Herb Vinegar	14, 16	●	●	●	●		●		46, 52
Honey Vinegar	14		●	●	●			●	40, 59, 61
Lemon Vinegar	13, 17	●	●	●	●		●	●	44, 46, 61
Malt Vinegar	15				●		●	●	60
Orange Vinegar	17	●	●	●	●		●		39, 40, 47, 59
Raspberry Vinegar	13, 16	●	●	●	●	●	●		43, 58
Red Wine Vinegar	9		●		●		●		10, 43, 47, 51, 52
Rice Vinegar	15		●		●		●		38, 42, 46
Shallot Vinegar	14, 16	●	●						44
Sherry Vinegar	11		●		●	●	●		36, 40, 48, 51
Sugar Cane Vinegar	15			●	●				58
Tarragon Vinegar	14, 16	●	●				●		39, 52
Truffle Vinegar	14		●			●			44
White Wine Vinegar	9		●	●	●	●	●		38, 39, 40, 44, 50, 56

R e c i p e

Oil	Page	Storing (Months)	Homemade	For Salads	For Drizzling on	For Marinating & Preserving	For Sauces	For Cooking	Used on Pages
Almond Oil	32	6		●	●				36
Chili Oil	34	6	●		●	●	●	●	37, 55
Corn Oil	28	10–18		●			●	●	38, 40, 43, 55
Garlic Oil	34	6	●	●		●	●	●	48
Ginger–Sweet Lime Oil	34	6	●	●	●	●			38
Grapeseed Oil	31	15		●				●	40
Hazelnut Oil	32	6		●	●				43
Herb Oil	34	6	●	●	●	●	●		44, 55
Linseed Oil	30	6		●					31
Olive Oil	22	18		●	●	●	●	●	36, 37, 40, 44, 48, 52, 54
Peanut Oil	32	18					●	●	52, 61
Pistachio Oil	32	6		●	●				36
Porcini Mushroom Oil	35	6	●	●	●		●		55
Pumpkinseed Oil	31	12		●	●				48
Rapeseed Oil	29	6–18		●				●	40, 47
Safflower Oil	30	12		●					40
Sesame Oil	32	18		●	●		●		42
Soy Oil	29	12		●			●	●	40, 42, 58, 60
Sunflower Oil	28	12–18		●	●		●	●	38, 40, 44, 47, 50
Walnut Oil	32	12		●	●	●			40, 43
Wheat Germ Oil	30	8		●	●				40

Vinegar– the Sour "Can Do it All"

Nowadays, in a gourmet's kitchen, one finds not only a variety of different oils, but also many different kinds of vinegars. New creations of noble sour liquids are constantly being added, and some gently flavored ones are even sipped as an apéritif or digestif. The color palette of the many varieties of vinegar is a large and vibrant one: From deep brown balsamic vinegar to bright red burgundy vinegar to pale yellow rice vinegar—there are a great many to choose from.

The Principle of Vinegar Production

Every type of vinegar contains alcohol. If for instance, wine is left standing, it will become sour. At some point, a gelatinous mass will swim on top, the so-called vinegar mother. Experts then speak of biological fermentation, which works in the following manner: There are always vinegar bacteria in the air, which settle on the liquid and change the alcohol into acetic acid. For this to take place, oxygen, which comes from the air, is needed.

When vinegar is produced, fermentation occurs in a controlled manner, in large tubs with very specific vinegar cultures.

Only a very high-grade vinegar is suitable as an apéritif or digestif: Here is a glass of the traditional vinegar, balsamic vinegar.

The Subtle Differences

Taste and quality of biologically obtained vinegar depends on the original products. Fermented apple wine tastes different than grape wine. And a late vintage produces higher-grade vinegar than table wine. Through storage in a wooden barrel, the vinegar gains enormous flavor. Also, the different vinegars are not equally sour in taste. Mild fruit and malt vinegars barely have five percent acidity, while wine vinegars, on the other hand, contain six to seven percent acidity.

In *Distilled Vinegar*, agrarian alcohol is fermented from sugar beets, grain, or potatoes. It is sold as "Table Vinegar" or "Dining Vinegar," and tastes sour without the slightest trace of flavor.

Wine-Distilled Vinegar consists of a mixture of at least one-quarter pure wine vinegar and three quarters distilled vinegar. It is used in many parts of the world.

Vinegar Concentrate has nothing to do with biological vinegar. It is a chemical-synthetic product with an acid content of 25 percent. As it is entirely without flavor, it is not used in cooking, and rightfully has been set aside for use in the cleaning corner.

Vinegar— The Sour Favorite

About 5000 years ago in ancient China, vinegar was an important means for preserving food. Among Roman legionnaires and farmers, vinegar water was once considered a refreshing thirst quencher. To this day vinegar demonstrates its all-round talent: It lends a sour flair to salads, tenderizes meat, and seasons both cold and warm sauces. The sour magician still preserves pickles, pumpkin, and carrots, but no longer out of the pure necessity for preserving, rather for the love of flavor.

Different in looks and above all in taste: Asian rice vinegar, French wine vinegar, and Italian balsamic vinegar.

Tips and Tricks

With the everyday work in the kitchen, vinegar is a real helper as well.

In preparation of:
Fish: Wrap the fish in a cloth seeped in vinegar, before putting it in the refrigerator, and it will keep fresh longer.

In preparation of:
Vegetables and Legumes: With a shot of vinegar in the cooking water, cauliflower will stay appetizingly white. Red cabbage on the other hand retains its nice red color with the addition of a bit of vinegar. Asparagus stays fresh longer in a towel dampened with vinegar water. A shot of vinegar added to lentils and beans not only gives them a fine flavor, but it also makes them easier to digest. But always add the vinegar at the very end, otherwise it lengthens the cooking time.

Balsamic Vinegar

It is the king among vinegars, especially when dealing with the traditional balsamic vinegar. It is produced only in small amounts in Italy's North provinces of Modena and Reggio Emilia—and it costs a fortune. No wonder, for when it arrives at the specialty stores in its round flacons with 0.1 liter content, it is at least 12 years old—the older, the more valuable. A little less expensive, and also available in good qualities, is the balsamic vinegar of Modena. The differences are in the production and, especially, in the ripening time.

Traditional Balsamic Vinegar

For this noble vinegar a special grape is used: The Trebbiano grape. These grapes are white and sweet, and are picked as late as possible. That's when the sugar content is especially high, and the flavor well developed. The grapes are ground and pressed. But the grape juice, also called cider, is not fermented into wine as is done with regular wine vinegar. Before it begins to ferment, it is placed in special kettles where the grape juice gently simmers. During that process, the consistency becomes rather thick, the sugar content higher, and the flavor more concentrated. Then begins the real, precise ritual: The filtered cider concentrate is poured into a special barrel, usually oak. There the alcoholic fermentation takes its course. The alcohol that develops is then changed into vinegar by acetic acid bacteria. In the course of the next years, the vinegar travels through a battery of smaller and smaller barrels of the most varied woods. They are made of chestnut, cherry, ash, mulberry, and juniper. While ripening, the vinegar takes on the flavor of the respective wood, and in that way develops its very specific aroma. How long it stays in each specific barrel is usually a strictly guarded secret of the producer's family. After 12 years, the day finally comes: For the first time the vinegar may be taken. From the original 70 quarts of grape cider only about 3 quarts of balsamic vinegar is produced. Some vinegars still ripen for decades longer. Before the noble vinegar can be sold, it has to pass a strict control of the consortium, an organization of the producers. Only then can it be filled into the specially designed round flacons, and sold with the corresponding control number. Gourmets reach deep into their pockets for this—a small bottle costs at least fifty dollars—and they dose out the elixir only by drops with a pipette.

For top-quality balsamic vinegar, the vinegar ripens in small barrels.

Non-Traditional Balsamic Vinegar

Considerably more affordable is non-traditional balsamic vinegar. It is available in delicatessens and supermarkets. It is merchandised as "Aceto Balsamico di Modena" from Italy. Some wineries in many countries throughout Europe offer outstanding vinegar or related products, often as direct sales. The big difference in comparison to the "Tradizionale" lies in the fact that the concepts of Aceto Balsamico and balsamic vinegar are not protected, and the production can vary greatly. Frequently they are produced from grape cider, which has already begun to ferment, or may be a mixture of old and young wine vinegars. In the worst case it is a wine vinegar, dyed brown with caramel color. Usually the price is an indicator of the quality. The more expensive vinegars may be of outstanding quality which, similarly to the "Tradizionale," have ripened in wooden barrels and have developed a full flavor.

The Flavor

In this non-traditional balsamic vinegar, delicate sour flavor harmonizes with tender sweetness and, depending on the product, may have an intense wood flavor or fruity bouquet.

The Use

The "Tradizionale" with its highly concentrated aroma is used only sparingly, dosed out drop by drop. You can be a little more generous with the non-traditional balsamic vinegar or "Aceto Balsamico de Modena." The possibilities for usage are quite varied. Here are a few suggestions:

• for strong vinaigrettes, which complement tomatoes, arugula, poultry, lentils and green salads, it is delicious combined with olive oil or walnut oil

• as enhancement for cold or warm sauces and dressings, also for seasoning gravies made with roast drippings, such as rabbit, calf's liver, beef, or lamb

• for dribbling on carpaccio or smoked duck breast, with Parma ham and melon

• for seasoning risotto

• for drizzling on fruit salads or strawberries as dessert

• top qualities used as apéritif or digestif mixed, if desired, with soda or mineral water

Quick Recipes with Balsamic Vinegar

• Spread very thinly sliced Parmesan on toasted slices of white bread, and sprinkle with balsamic vinegar and olive oil.

• Wash radishes, trim, and slice thin. Sauté for 2 minutes in heated sunflower oil. Add a bit of balsamic vinegar. Season with salt and pepper, and sprinkle with chopped fresh parsley. This makes a good antipasta.

• Slice red onions and sauté in plenty of olive oil. Add balsamic vinegar. Season with salt and pepper. Serve as an antipasta.

Delicacies for
Italian antipasta

Wine Vinegar

At one time, the relationship between winegrowers and vinegar was a rather unhappy one. If the laboriously produced wine suddenly turned out to be sour, this was a devastating failure for the winegrower. During transport the wine would sometimes spoil, perhaps on the way from a winery in Bordeaux to the markets in Paris. The result was a new branch of the profession, which started in the middle of the 18th century, the vinaigriers: The vinegar merchants in the harbor of Orleans. There the unhappy winegrower was able to sell his wine and, little by little, the vinegar makers succeeded in producing extremely tasty kinds of vinegar. French cooks soon began to appreciate vinegars as a delicate seasoning. The triumphal march of wine vinegar into gourmet kitchens took its course from then on.

The Production of Wine Vinegar

It has been a long time now since wine vinegar has emerged from a chance product to a quality product. Different procedures take place during the fermentation process of turning wine into vinegar. Vinegar bacteria and oxygen are always involved in the fermentation process. The so-called Orleans procedure developed by the French vinegar makers is not widely used today. In this procedure, wine and a small amount of wine vinegar were put into a barrel. Through special openings, air could stream in and out. On the surface of the barrel, where the "vinegar mother" builds up, the acetic acid fermentation takes place. The acetic acid sinks to the bottom. For that reason, vinegar is drawn off at the bottom, while on top, new wine is filled in. This process is extremely time consuming, but it does produce high-quality vinegar varieties.

Nowadays, vinegar is usually produced in vinegar makers, called "acetators." Here the vinegar bacteria move around freely in the tub with the wine. Air is constantly blown into the tub. This supplies the bacteria with the necessary oxygen. Airflow and temperatures are strictly regulated, and are often computer directed. Experts call this method of vinegar making the submerse procedure. The results are high-quality vinegars. A fast vinegar procedure that uses beech shavings usually is employed only for the less expensive distilled vinegars. In this method, the alcohol containing liquid trickles over wood shavings, which have been inoculated with vinegar bacteria. In vinegar production as a rule, the longer the vinegar fermentation takes, the better and more aromatic the vinegar will be. With some producers this procedure can take over a year.

From Young Vinegar to Top Product

The result of the vinegar fermentation is always a raw product. The young or raw vinegar must be stored, so that particles can settle, and the characteristic aroma can develop. If it is high-quality wine vinegar, then it is transferred into wooden barrels, often oak. There the vinegar ripens, sometimes for many years. In order for the vinegar to become clear, it flows through a filter before it is put into bottles. Some specialties are marketed as unfiltered.

The higher quality the wine, the better the vinegar: Wine barrels in Frankonia.

The Use of Red and White Wine Vinegar

There are as many possibilities for use as there are varieties of vinegar. Principally, one differentiates between red and white wine vinegar. This is not only a question of color, but also one of taste. Vinegar made from white wine tastes rather mild, and vinegar made from red wine has a stronger taste.

White Wine Vinegar is Suitable:

• for vinaigrette with mild green salads, asparagus, shrimp, fish

• for light raw vegetables

• for salads with cooked vegetables, such as potatoes, carrots, cauliflower

• for mayonnaise

• for preserving fruit, vegetables, fish

Red Wine Vinegar is Suitable:

• for vinaigrettes with strong green salads, such as friseé or lamb's lettuce

• for salads made with cooked vegetables such as leek, savoy cabbage, red cabbage

• for preserving beef roast, or game, and for seasoning gravies made from roast drippings

In the Trend: German Winegrowers' Vinegar

While vinegar culture has been progressing for quite a while in France, it now is beginning to get a foothold in Germany as well. Numerous winegrowers have begun to produce high-grade vinegar from their late Burgundy, Riesling, or Gewürztra-

Vineyard in Martins Valley

miner wines. Only a good wine can make a good vinegar. Even high-quality wine made from selected grapes is now being used in the most noble vinegars. Read the label, and you'll often find the place of origin, the kind of grapes, and at times, the year and acidity content. By law, vinegar has to be at least six percent acid for it to be considered a pure wine vinegar.

The New Vinegar Culture

Nowadays, the noble vinegars can be found in stylish containers. Many a pre-

cious elixir can be found bottled in a well-designed and extravagant carafe. Artistic labels also help to make the optical effect perfect. And that is not all: Special long stemmed glasses are available for the enjoyment of the vinegar apéritif or digestif. And in case the vinegar is meant to lend its aroma only slightly to carpaccio, salmon, or other delicate foods, there is a vinegar sprayer made of glass.

The Noble Wine Vinegars

Late Burgundy, Gewürz-traminer, or Riesling vinegars are elixirs that are rich in aroma. Some are additionally enriched in flavor with spices and fruits. This idea is not new. In ancient times street venders offered vinegars that were infused with spices and berries. Here are a few examples of today's popular vinegars, and the many uses for these noble liquids.

• late Burgundy vinegar: For strong salad dressings, to use with oak leaf lettuce, radicchio, red cabbage, and for gravies made from roast drippings

• late Burgundy vinegar with bay leaves: For strong pickling solution used in preserving game and beef

• late Burgundy vinegar with chestnut honey: For goose liver, or for seasoning fruity dessert salads, such as those with peaches and pears

• Gewürztraminer vinegar: Ideal with carpaccio served with some thinly sliced smoked salmon

• Riesling vinegar: For fish marinades and sauces, for vinaigrettes with green salads, or with asparagus

• Beerenauslese vinegar from Germany: Cold as an apéritif or digestif

• White wine vinegar with strawberries: For sweet-sour marinating of fruit, and for use with raw vegetable salads.

Vinegar Jelly

It is worthwhile to try out new vinegar specialties, and to experiment with them. For example, try the following extraordinary recipe: In a pot, slightly heat 4 cups late Burgundy vinegar with chestnut honey, and dissolve 2 envelopes gelatin in the warm vinegar. (Or use a good red wine vinegar and 1 tsp honey.) Pour the liquid into a shallow, rectangular dish. Let it solidify in the refrigerator. Cut it into small cubes with a knife. Vinegar jelly goes particularly well with salads served as hors d'oeuvres, for instance with lamb's lettuce or wild herbs. It is also a wonderful accompaniment to goose liver in puff pastry shells.

As a variation you can prepare a light jelly with less acidity if you mix 2 cups Gewürztraminer vinegar, or a good white vine vinegar, with 2 cups freshly pressed, strained orange juice. Prepare the jelly as described above.

Vinegar jelly is not only an attractive visual addition to salads, but it also tastes exquisite, for instance, with puff pastries.

Sherry Vinegar

Sherry Vinegar

The southwest region of Spain is considered the home of sherry. The town of Jerez de la Frontera is the birthplace of the world famous sherry vinegar, the "Vinaigre de Jerez."

The sweet taste in the sherry vinegar comes from sherry wines. All around Jerez, on especially low growing vines, you can find white sweet grapes thriving, mostly of the Palimino variety. Before the grapes are pressed, they are dried in the sun. That way the sugar content rises, and the wine is particularly sweet. Sherry wines are not stored in cellars, but in gigantic cathedral-like halls with mighty vaults, called Bodegas. During the day, thick walls serve as protection against the Andalusian heat. During the night, a breeze provides cooling through open roof hatches. The barrels lie stacked on top of each other, and in a cleverly thought out system, the young sherries are stored in the top barrels. These young sherries are eventually transferred into the barrels just below them, then more young sherries are added into the top barrels. The barrels are filled only three quarters with wine. On the surface, a so-called "flor" (or flower) develops. This is the yeast, which is supposed to protect the sherry against vinegar fermentation. In vinegar production, on the other hand, vinegar bacteria are added to the sherry wines on purpose. The ripening of the sherry vinegar proceeds exactly as that of the sherry itself. The vinegar travels through several oak barrels from top to bottom, and the top qualities take up to 30 years to complete the process.

Color and Flavor

Sherry vinegar can be dark brown, honey, light brown, or a shimmering reddish color. Usually, the stronger the color, the more intense the flavor. The aroma is a mixture of wood and fruit tones. The acidity content is between six and eight percent for this type of sherry. Sherry vinegar contains remnants of alcohol, below one percent.

Use

As sherry vinegar has a very concentrated taste, it should be used sparingly. In vinaigrettes it harmonizes beautifully with olive oil, walnut oil, or hazelnut oil. Sherry vinegar goes well with strong salads such as lamb's lettuce or endive, as well as with tomatoes and arugula. It pairs well with lentil dishes and—drizzled on in drops—gives smoked duck breast a special flair. Sherry vinegar is ideal for marinating dark meat, but can also be used for fish, such as a young herring fillet. And even cheese receives an entirely new flavor component (see page 48). It also enhances the taste of gravies and tomato soup.

Sherry barrels in the Osborne Estate in Spain

Fruit Vinegar

If the label says fruit vinegar, it is usually apple vinegar. For other fruit vinegar specialties, the fruit is usually mentioned, for instance raspberry vinegar.

Apple Vinegar

It has always had the reputation for being healthful vinegar. For this reason, apple vinegar is mostly offered in the health sections of supermarkets, or in health food stores. But by now, gourmets have also discovered it. The production follows the same principle as for wine vinegar. The main product in this vinegar is apples, which are pressed and then fermented into apple wine.

Vinegar bacteria change the alcohol into acetic acid. Since the alcohol content of apple wine is lower than that of wine, less acid develops as well. As a rule it is five percent acid. The aroma of the vinegar depends on the type of apple from which it was produced. The more tasty the apples, the more aromatic the vinegar. A specialty from France is the cider vinegar. As its name indicates, it is produced from the sweet-sour cider apples. Usually apple vinegar is filtered, and sometimes briefly heated to make it less perishable. Some types of apple vinegar are available unfiltered.

Flavor
Fruity, dry apple flavor and mild acidity are among the distinguishing tastes in this vinegar.

Use
For vinaigrettes, butter lettuce and other tender lettuces, raw vegetables like celery or carrots, and marinades for poultry, or fish. Apple vinegar is also suitable for the morning drink (see recipe above), or for making chutneys.

The Morning Drink
This will wake you up! Mix 2 tbs fruit vinegar with 1 tbs honey. Add mineral water and stir.

Fruit Vinegar for Health and Beauty

The mild fruit vinegar gains its taste from apples, and is among the ancient remedies used in folk medicine. It contains all the valuable minerals from the apple, including lots of potassium.

Apple vinegar has a particularly favorable effect on a balanced acid base relationship in the body. Taken regularly, perhaps as a wake-up drink in the morning using the above recipe, it will stimulate the metabolism and aid digestion. Vinegar can also be used in the tub, for a refreshing, fragrant bath.

Apples, lemons, and raspberries produce tasty and explicitly healthy vinegars.

A mouth rinse with vinegar water (3 tbs vinegar per 8-oz glass water) is considered a good remedy for bleeding gums, bad breath, and tartar. If your hair is dull you should give vinegar a try: A little fruit vinegar added to the last rinse gives your hair a silky shine.

Raspberry Vinegar

It is enticing both in color and in taste. Raspberry vinegar is usually flavor-enriched wine or fruit vinegar. It tastes quite delicious, and one can easily make it at home (see pages 16–17).

Pure fruit vinegar is a real treat: Freshly pressed raspberry juice is fermented to make wine, and afterwards, with the aid of vinegar bacteria, it is made into raspberry vine-gar. This specialty is rarely found, and not inexpensive. Some vinegar producers also offer pure fruit vinegar made from currents, blackberries, blueberries, or peaches.

Flavor
Fruit vinegars have a distinct fruit aroma, depending on the fruit used, and they are also mildly acidic.

Use
For vinaigrettes on light summer salads, such as salads of tender greens topped with poultry. They also taste great on lukewarm salads with duck breast or lentils. Try them for marinating beets, or serve them with fruit salads. Thinned with water, they make a refreshing summer drink or apéritif.

Lemon Vinegar

This is always a flavor enhanced wine or fruit vinegar. To make it yourself, see page 17.

A good start for the day is our Morning Drink (left, in the photo). On hot days this summer drink is delicious (right, in the photo).

Aromatic Vinegars

Spices and herbs enrich wine and fruit vinegars in various and tasty ways. Aromatic vinegar specialties can be made at home with little effort and are inexpensive (see pages 16-17). Here is an overview of the most common kinds on the market.

Tarragon Vinegar

This is a classic of French cuisine. Its spicy aroma is similar to anise, and it is extremely versatile in its use. You can read more about this vinegar, see page 16.

Herb Vinegar

The selection of herb vinegars, usually made with white wine vinegar, is huge. Oregano vinegar, basil vinegar, mint vinegar, dill vinegar, parsley vinegar, etc., are just a few of the varieties. The herb mixture usually determines the aroma.

Use
Oregano and basil vinegar go well with salads that have tomatoes, peppers, or zucchini. Mint vinegar tastes good with tender green lettuce and in combination with fruit. Dill vinegar enhances pickle, herring, egg, and potato salads, and is appropriate for pickling cucumbers. Parsley vinegar is suitable for potato, poultry, meat, and vegetable salads.

Honey Vinegar

This is an extremely mild vinegar made with wine or fruit vinegar. A special and noble variety is late Burgundy vinegar with chestnut honey (see page 10). Uncommonly rare are vinegars fermented from honey wine.

Use
Honey vinegar goes with vinaigrettes both on green and wild green salads, as well as with raw vegetables such as carrots, celery, and red cabbage.

Bay Leaf Vinegar

This is the right mixture for everyone who likes bay leaves. Frequently the vinegar is given additional sharpness from white or black peppercorns. You can get bay leaf vinegar made from white wine or red wine vinegar.

Use
Bay leaf vinegar is used for preserving game and roast beef, for seasoning dark, strong gravies, or one-dish meals with lentils or beans. It is also appropriate for red cabbage, and beet dishes.

Shallot Vinegar

You can forget bothersome onion chopping; the shallot vinegar brings an intense and unique onion taste to the table.

Use
Shallot vinegar is good in vinaigrettes on green salads, but also can be used for potato salads or salads with legumes or noodles.

Truffle Vinegar

This exclusive specialty calls for a high-grade vinegar, such as sherry vinegar.

Use
The intense truffle aroma goes especially well with goose liver in puff pastry. But truffle vinegar can also turn a wintry green salad with fresh mushrooms into an extraordinary delicacy.

Walnut Vinegar

Wine vinegar with a delicate walnut aroma enhanced with herbs.

Use
Walnut vinegar is ideal in vinaigrettes with strong greens such as lamb's lettuce or arugula, and also for preserving game.

International Vinegar Specialties

Whether you are in the Caribbean, Japan, or elsewhere in the world, vinegar can probably be found in most countries. Most people swear their local variety is a sour treat. Some types of vinegar are hard to find, but are usually available in shops specializing in oil and vinegar, or in a well-stocked delicatessen. If you're out on a shopping trip or traveling, and you discover a special vinegar, there is only one thing to do: Go for it, and test it.

Beer Vinegar

A specialty from Southern Germany with a spicy beer taste. The light yellow or dark brown vinegar goes perfectly with gravies for pork roast. It seasons lentil dishes, and lends a special flair to raw vegetables such as radish or sauerkraut.

Rice Vinegar

Vinegar is also an important element on rice, the bread of Asia. The Japanese rice vinegar is transparent, and tastes very mild. A must for sushi rice. The Thai variant is also transparent and mild. The Thai use it to marinate vegetables, poultry, and fish. The Chinese rice vinegar is dark brown and tastes strongly like soy sauce

and malt. It is suitable for marinating duck, and is used for dark gravies and as a dip.

Coconut Vinegar

The vinegar in the Philippines is milky cloudy, and tastes sweet and sour. The delicate aroma of the coconut harmonizes with strongly spiced vegetable dishes and with seafood.

Malt Vinegar

This classic from England is a must with "fish &

From coconut and walnuts, herbs, shallots, honey, and rice to beer: These products make outstanding vinegars.

chips." In addition, this brown vinegar with the sweet-sour taste and the unmistakable malt aroma goes with chutneys, and in dark gravies made from roast drippings.

Sugar Cane Vinegar

The light brown to reddish vinegar tastes intensely sour, and tastes a lot like sugar cane. It is appropriate for pairing with sweet and exotic fruits, for example papayas (see pages 58–59).

Homemade Spice Vinegars

You can give aroma to vinegar with herbs, berries, spices, or blossoms without much effort. Make sure that the seasoned ingredients are always well covered with vinegar. Tightly closed and stored in a cool place, the vinegar specialties will keep up to one year. With the exception of fruit vinegars, such as raspberry, lemon, or orange vinegar, which at most will keep for six months. Then they can spoil or, at least, lose some aroma.

Tarragon Vinegar

3 sprigs fresh tarragon
2 cups white wine vinegar

1 Wash tarragon, spin dry, and dry well in a kitchen towel. Place the sprigs in a clean bottle.

2 Heat vinegar in a pot, and pour over the herbs. Close the bottle. Allow the vinegar to stand on a windowsill for 2-3 weeks. Then remove the herbs, chop them, and use for seasoning (see below).

Use
• for sauce, Bearnaise (see page 39)
• for vinaigrettes with green salads, such as butter lettuce or frisée, or with egg, poultry, or meat salads
• for fish sauces
• for potato soups
• for mayonnaise, ideal with fish or shrimp

VARIATIONS

Instead of tarragon, you can make herb vinegar with dill, mint, lemon balm, or parsley.

Garlic Vinegar

12 cloves garlic
1/2 tsp salt
2 cups white wine vinegar

1 Peel garlic, chop coarsely, place in a bowl and sprinkle with salt.

2 Bring vinegar to boiling, and pour over the garlic. Let it stand, covered, at room temperature, for 1 week. Then pour through a strainer, and with the aid of a funnel, pour into a clean bottle.

Use
• for vinaigrettes with green salads, fish salad, and tomato salad
• for marinated, cooked vegetables, such as eggplant, zucchini, or mushrooms
• for chutneys
• for hearty one-dish meals

VARIATIONS

Shallot Vinegar:
Quarter 5 small shallots, salt them, and pour red wine vinegar over them. Proceed further as with the Garlic Vinegar recipe.

Raspberry Vinegar

3/4 cup fresh or frozen raspberries
1 2/3 cups fruit vinegar

1 Sort fresh raspberries and put in a wide-neck jar or bottle. Pour vinegar over the raspberries.

2 Let the vinegar stand for 1 week. Then pour it through a strainer, lined with a clean cloth. With the aid of a funnel, pour the raspberry vinegar into a clean bottle.

3 Press out the raspberries in the cloth. Pour this liquid separately into a glass, and use as soon as possible, for example as a summer drink (see page 13).

Use
• for vinaigrettes with green salads, and for drizzling on smoked duck breast
• for game gravies
• for salads with fruits
• for zippy drinks

Lemon Vinegar

3 lemons (1 of
these organic)
1¹/₃ cups fruit vinegar

1 Cut off the peel of the organic lemon in spiral form. Squeeze the juice from all 3 lemons. The yield should be about ¹/₂ cup juice.

2 Mix the lemon juice and peel with the vinegar in a bottle. Let stand for 1 week. Pour the vinegar through a fine strainer, and pour into a clean bottle. If desired, return the lemon peel to the vinegar bottle.

Use
• for vinaigrettes with crisp summer salads
• for mayonnaise with fish or seafood

VARIATIONS

Orange Vinegar:
Mix ¹/₂ cup freshly squeezed orange juice and orange peel spiral from an organic orange with 1¹/₃ cups white wine vinegar. Proceed as with Lemon Vinegar recipe. For sauce (see Bearnaise, page 39), for preserving fruit (see pages 58–59), and for vinaigrette with carrot and fennel salad.

Blossom Vinegar

1 handful blossoms
(lavender, rose, borage,
or elder blossoms from
the garden, not sprayed,
or from the florist!)
1¹/₃ cups white
wine vinegar

1 Place the blossoms into a wide-neck bottle. Pour wine vinegar over them.

2 Let the vinegar stand at room temperature for 1 week. Then pour through a strainer, and into a clean bottle.

Use
• for vinaigrettes with bitter or wild lettuces
• for salads with fruit
• for Vinegar Jelly
(see page 10)

From top to bottom:
Lemon vinegar, garlic
vinegar, raspberry vinegar,
tarragon vinegar, and
blossom vinegar.

Variety of Oils

The variety of different oils has never been as large as it is today. One thing is common to all: The origin is always botanical. Oil is pressed from fruits such as olives, as well as from seeds. Fats are the natural energy reserves of plants, and are important for the development and nutritional supply for the seedling. What nourishes the plant sprout is also a good energy source for humans. Plant oils, as well as any other fats, are rich in energy (nine calories per gram), and they enrich the food with vitamin E and essential fatty acids. This effect varies depending on the oil used. Each type of oil has its own advantages in terms of nutrition, taste, and use. For that reason, oil connoisseurs have many choices.

Oil is a Good Aroma Carrier

Fat is always an aroma enhancer. Oil, as any fat, is in itself an aroma carrier, and it enhances the inherent flavor of the ingredients. Depending on the choice of oil, you can consciously control taste accents by deciding on a flavor intensive oil, or on an oil with a more neutral taste. In addition, oil readily absorbs other aromas, for example the flavor of herbs and spices. How about trying a herb or chili oil (see pages 34–35).

The Subtle Difference: The Fatty Acids

How healthy an oil is depends on its structure. Like all fats, oil consists of glycerin and various fatty acids. The differences are a question of chemistry. The combination of the individual atoms in a fatty acid plays an essential role. The most important thing here are the double bonds in the molecule. Fatty acids without any double bonds are called saturated. Those with a double bond are simply called unsaturated. Also important is the oil acidity. Further, there are polyunsaturated fatty acids, such as linoleic acid with two double bonds, and linoleic acid with three. Polyunsaturated fatty acids can not usually be produced by the human metabolism itself. Therefore they must be, as with vitamins, taken with food. Polyunsaturated fatty acids are also called essential fatty acids; that is, they are essential for living. They are indispensable for the functioning of our metabolism. When looking at oil bottle labels, you have probably noticed the following description: "Particularly rich in essential, polyunsaturated fatty acids." In such oils, more than 50 percent of the entire fatty acids consist of linoleic acid. An overview of the structure of the individual oils is found in the chart on page 33.

Fatty Acids and Cholesterol Level

Polyunsaturated fatty acids lower the cholesterol level in the blood. Monounsaturated fatty acids also have a favorable effect on the cholesterol level by decreasing the cholesterol deposits in the blood vessels. Saturated fatty acids usually increase the cholesterol level in the blood. The great plus of oils: They contain practically no cholesterol. A few sprout oils, for instance, corn oil contain sitosterin, which prevents the absorption of cholesterol in the body.

Oil Brings and Frees Vitamins

The most important oil vitamin is vitamin E. This fat soluble vitamin is a protective factor for the unsaturated fatty acids in the oil. It contributes to keeping the fatty acids in the oil intact, so they do not get destroyed through oxidation. They prevent oil from getting rancid. As vitamin E is light sensitive, oils should be filled into dark bottles or cans, or at least, be stored in a dark place. Vitamin E also has a protective function in the body: As a so-called antioxidant or radical absorbent, it protects the human cells. It plays a role in cancer prevention and protects against arterioscleroses. It is recommended that 12 mg of vitamin E be consumed each day. The body needs fat in order to evenly absorb the other fat-soluble vitamins —namely A, D, and K. Oil, thus brings the vitamins in salads and vegetables out of the reserve, and makes them available.

Oil is available in many varied bottles and sizes. Oils in light glass bottles should definitely be stored in a dark place.

Oil Production

Romantic oil mills with their aura of nostalgia are a part of the past. Today the oil seeds and fruits, which originate in various parts of the world, are being processed with the most modern methods. A quick look behind the scenes of a modern oil mill illustrates how table oil is produced from the seeds.

Cold Pressed Oils

They are the favorites of gourmets and whole food enthusiasts. This is how they are produced: The oil seeds are cleaned and crushed. After that they go into a press in the form of a snail, which is run automatically. The oil that is produced goes through a filter, and after that, into the bottle. Done! The concept of cold pressed or cold beaten, by the way, cannot be taken entirely literally as during the pressing process some heat is produced. Sometimes the seeds or kernels are slightly roasted during pressing, for instance in pumpkin and sesame seed oil. The oil gets an espe-cially intense flavor that way. Refining, as described below, is in not permitted with cold pressed oils. A mild steam treatment, however, is not necessarily excluded. This is usually not declared on the label. For olive oil, there are very clearly defined regu-lations (see pages 22-27)

More Tips on Cold Pressed Oils

Left in their natural state, oils keep their true fruit or seed flavor. The natural vitamin content is higher. The seeds must fulfill high-quality demands.

Cold pressed, unrefined oils however, do not keep as long, and they are con-siderably more expensive than the refined ones.

Use

Cold pressed oils are ideal for salads, raw vegetables, and for use in marinating foods. For vegetables, it is best to drizzle oil over them only after cooking. Cold pressed oils should never be heated too much, so they are there-fore not recommended for roasting and frying.

An oil mill in Italy: Clearly recognizable are the rotating millstones.

TIP!

The intense, intrinsic flavor of some cold pressed oils can be rather unconventional. Buy a small bottle at first and try it.

Refined Oils

The first step here, as with the cold pressed oils, is the pressing. During this process, rather high temperatures occur. If there is still fat in the seeds after pressing, then through the special process of extraction, the last drop of oil is removed. This is done with the aid of a solvent, which is completely removed again afterwards. The oil gained in this way is called raw oil. Raw oil can have undesired fatty acids and impurities, which negatively effect taste and look. For this reason, a several-step refining process takes place. During this process, the impurities are removed with hot water and centrifugal force, and the free fatty acids are neutralized. Through bleaching, undesired color components are removed. The so-called deodorizing makes the oils free of unwanted odor and flavor components, and removes any remaining residue. This takes place with steam. A further step can be the so-called winterizing process that prevents any later clumping in the refrigerator.

Are Refined Oils Inferior?

The content of the polyunsaturated fatty acids is hardly altered by refining; therefore, these oils are not any worse to our health than cold pressed oils. However, the vitamin E content is reduced. For that reason, some producers add vitamin E. The species-specific taste and the natural color of the oil, however, are lost after this treatment. Therefore, refined oils usually taste neutral and are light yellow.

Use

Refined oils are ideal for roasting, braising, frying and whenever distinctive oil aroma is not desired. As these oils are neutral in flavor, they are ideal for mixing with oils that have a more intense flavor, for instance in a vinaigrette with nut oils or pumpkin seed oil.

Storage Tips

* True for all oils: Store in a cool and dark place. Oxygen, light, and warmth promote the decomposition of the substances, and the oil becomes rancid. Choose oils in dark bottles, or cans! They are considerably better if they are protected from light.

• Opened oil bottles should always be closed tightly, and are best stored in a refrigerator. If possible, use within two or three months.

• Unrefined oils do not keep as long as refined oils. Therefore it is recommended to buy these oils in small quantities. The specific length of time the oil may be kept is given in the description of the individual oils. Once unrefined oils are opened, they should be used up fairly soon.

• Oil stored in the refrigerator, especially unrefined oil, can form flakes. This is a natural process, and has no influence on the quality. Take the oil bottle out of the refrigerator a few minutes before use. At room temperature the flakes will quickly dissolve.

• When buying oil, look for the date: "eat by..." or "best before..." It indicates the minimum date, and how long the oil will keep, unopened, when properly stored. If it is past the date, it does not mean the product has to be thrown out immediately—this is not an expiration date. If the oil does not smell or taste rancid, then it can certainly be used.

Olive Oil

The oil with the oldest cultural history is quite special. It can hardly be surpassed in facet variety. The color palette alone ranges from light yellow to dark green. The scent varies from very tender to extremely intense. But most exciting is the flavor. Olive oil can taste almost sweet, or bitter, fruity, or rather nutty, or very strong or mild. Connoisseurs with a fine tongue can even distin-guish aromas of artichokes, bananas, or apples. Similar to wine, the variety, origin, region, and climate all determine the character of the oils.

The classic olive countries around the Mediterranean Sea knew how to appre-ciate this wonderful tree even during the earliest centuries. Already in antiq-uity, olive oil was not only one of the staple foods, but was also a balsam for head and hair, a healing remedy and, as an impor-tant light source, it was burned in oil lamps.

The origin of the olive tree was found in the Near East. There it already had flourished for 6000 years. Thanks to Phoenician merchants, the tree came to Europe. The oil tree has its place even in the bible. Thus, Noah's dove returned to the arc with an oil branch. The Greeks call the oil "nectar of the gods," and the olive tree is dedicated to the goddess Athena. On vases from antiquity are brilliant depictions of how the precious oil is obtained from the olive fruits. In principle, hardly anything has changed in that process to this day.

Olives—the Sun Fruits

Long, dry summers, lots of sunshine, and only a few days of frost are the optimal conditions for the evergreen olive trees with the silvery shimmering leaves. These trees can reach the biblical age of over 100 years. The mild Mediterranean climate is perfect for the gnarled trees. Italy, Spain, Greece, France, and Portugal are home to at least 50 kinds of olive trees, which pro-duce fruits with entirely different flavors. The variety of shapes range from round to oval to pointed. The size ranges from tiny to very large. Between April and June the olive groves are trans-formed into a lovely fra-grant sea of blossoms. From about 100 white-yellow blossoms, only about five stone fruits develop. They change

An olive grove in Italy during the spring.

color from green to dark violet to black. Thus the color has nothing to do with the species, but with the degree of ripeness. During the ripening phase, the oil develops in the fruits: The content varies between 15 and 75 percent.

The Harvest

Mid-October to mid-March is harvest time for the olive trees. This depends on the climate and region. The time of harvest effects the flavor. The early harvest of the still green olives delivers an oil with a tangy, slightly bitter flavor. The late harvest of the fully ripe fruit produces an oil with a sweetish, almost almond like aroma. To this day, the small fruits are laboriously picked into baskets by hand, particularly on the steep, rough hillsides. Handpicked fruits result in an oil of especially good quality. The harvest process is not quite as arduous if one lets the fruits fall onto nets or tarps, as it is if the fruits are shaken off the tree with sticks. The most efficient process is the

shaking machine, with nets that catch the olives immediately. Important for the quality of the oil: The fruits must get to the mill and under the press fairly quickly, and undamaged. Once the delicate skin and the actual olive fruit are hurt, the natural process of decomposition is set into motion. During that process an acid is produced, which has the effect of diminishing the quality. The less acid the olive oil contains later on, the more valuable and expensive it is.

A tree produces on average 44 lb of olives. From this, three to five quarts of olive oil are obtained from each tree.

Pressing

Olive oil is always cold pressed. This may be surprising to some, but warm pressing is indeed a relic of the past. Considerable amounts of oil were once left in the squashed olives after the first pressing. The oil mass was mixed with hot water, and pressed a second and third time. Meanwhile the presses have become so efficient, that in a single

Green, unripe olives, when pressed, produce a tangy, slightly bitter oil.

pressing, without the addition of heat, all the oil is pressed from the olives. Today, olive oil is produced in the following way:

First the harvested olive fruits are freed from branches and leaves, then they are washed. Now the fruits, complete with the stones, go into the actual

mill. It looks like a giant bowl. In it the millstones are rotating, and they grind the olives into a mush. Experts call this step the rumbling step. Now the olive mush is distributed on so-called mats. They look like round disks; in the middle is a whole. These mats are stacked on a kind of a pipe, and thus make a tower. The pressing today is usually done with the aid of the most advanced technology, with automatic, hydraulic presses. During pressing, through friction, some heat develops, but the temperature remains low. Through the intense pressure, a so-called emulsion is pressed out first. This is a mixture of oil, and fruit water. In order to obtain pure oil, the emulsion has to go into the centrifuge. The oil that flows out here is not the end product—it is still cloudy. Only after being filtered is the oil nice and clear, and ready to fill into bottles. For 1 qt of olive oil, 9 to 11 lb of fruit are needed. An

especially precious olive oil specialty is the dripped oil. The yield of this extraordinarily tasty oil is not particularly high. For 1 qt of oil, 24 lb of olives are required. Dripped oils frequently are available unfiltered. They taste especially fruity and mild.

The Quality Grades

The consumer demand for olive oils is immense. Which oil should I buy? Which is the best oil? First of all, you should study the label. Contrary to other oils, clear guidelines have been created for olive oil, regarding labeling. The criteria are flavor, scent, and color, as well as the content of free fatty

acids. The lower the percentage of free fatty acids, counted as oil acid, the better the grade.

Extra Virgin Olive Oil
The highest quality oil is obtained from fresh, high-grade olives. The amount of free fatty acids cannot be higher than 1/4 oz per 3 1/2 oz of olive oil. Extra virgin is a term used for valuable oil, and is specified on the label. In the case of particularly high-grade oils, the amount of the free fatty acids is often listed on the labels. If you read for example acid content 0.2 percent, you are dealing with a high-grade oil. Extra virgin olive oil cannot contain more than one percent acid.

Virgin Olive Oil
Not as high quality as extra virgin olive oil. Here the amount of free fatty acids can be up to 1/2 oz per 3 1/2 oz, and the acid content cannot exceed two percent.

Olive Oil
If the oil does not meet the criteria regarding color, taste, and scent, and if the content of free fatty acids is too high, then the oil gets refined. This oil is then mixed with virgin olive oil, in order to improve its flavor. The oil acidity content is 1/2 oz per 3 1/2 oz.

Color and Flavor
Olive oil shimmers in varied shades of yellow and green. But a strong color does not necessarily mean a strong flavor. There are strong green oils that taste extremely mild, and tender yellow ones with a surprisingly intense flavor. Sometimes the label will give an indication such as strong, fruity, or mild flavor. Other than that, there is only one thing to do: Try, try, try again, until

Italian olive oil, fresh from the press.
Note the intensive green color!

you have found your favorite olive oil. In specialty shops, merchants will be glad to assist you and maybe let you do some tasting.

Flavor and the Region

Similar to wine, the region where it is grown also plays an important role for olive oil. In addition, of course, factors such as variety, time of harvest, and year, matter as well. Most of the olive oils that can be purchased are from Italy or Spain.

Ripe black olives create oil with unmistakable aroma and taste.

Italian Olive Oils

In Italy one differentiates between the olive growing regions by North, Middle, and South. The oils from Italy's North come from the region around Lake Garda, from Liguria, Friuli, or Romagna. The flavor is mild and flowery. Italy's Middle region offers the greatest variety: Tuscany, Umbria, Latium, and their brands produce oils with a stronger flavor. Olive oils from the South, from Calabria, and from Apulia, are not exported as often and have a very intense, almost spicy flavor.

Spanish Olive Oils

Most of the olive trees thrive in the wide, hilly landscape of Andalusia. Another important region is Catalonia. The indication on the label "Denominacion Origen," short D.O., means that the oil is equivalent to the class "extra virgin olive oil." Other protected indications of origin are:

• "Borjas Blancas" for oils from Catalonia, province Lerida. A mild oil with a slightly nutty flavor.

• "Siurana" for oils from Catalonia, province Tarragona. A slightly stronger oil with a definite fruit flavor.

• "Baena" for Andalusian oils from Baena and Cordoba. An oil with a mild and fruity flavor.

• "Sierra de Segura" for Andalusian oil from the province Jaen. An especially strong, expressive oil, sometimes with a touch of bitterness.

Olive Oil and Health

The reputation of olive oil until recently was the following: Although the oil tastes excellent, it is not particularly healthy, since it has too few of the highly praised polyunsaturated fatty acids. Olive oil consists of almost 80 percent monounsaturated fatty acids, and for a long time these were not highly regarded because of their high cholesterol reading. But newer scientific findings have proven that olive oil is healthy. The high percentage of monounsaturated fatty acids has a positive effect on the cholesterol level. They lower the so-called bad LDL cholesterol, which deposits itself on the walls of the arteries, and at the same time, they contain the good HDL cholesterol, which removes cholesterol deposited on the walls of the arteries, and transports it to the liver, where it is rendered harmless. For this reason, olive oil protects against high cholesterol levels and high blood pressure. This might explain why there are fewer heart attacks in the Mediterranean countries than elsewhere in the world. Mediterranean cuisine uses plenty of olive oil as well as lots of vegetables, which are now regarded as a prime example of healthy nutrition: Consequently, olive oil gourmets and health conscious people can enjoy their favorite olive oils without any bad conscience.

Storing Olive Oil

The optimal way to store oil is in a cool, dark place. The olive oil should be protected from light. For that reason it is best stored in dark bottles or in a closed cupboard. If you put your olive oil in the refrigerator, don't get startled when you want to use it next, as lower temperatures make the oil flaky and cloudy. The quality is not diminished. At room temperature, the oil will quickly become clear again.

Olive oil "pure" is a pleasure. It is also excellent used with various spice oils (see page 34).

Shelf Life

Stored correctly, and unopened, olive oil keeps for at least 18 months. For the cloudy oils the time is less; they keep only one year at most. Once the bottle is opened, it should be closed tightly immediately after use, and be used up fairly soon.

Use

Olive oil is incredibly versatile. The possibilities for use are just about endless. Gourmets prefer the best quality grade, the extra virgin olive oil.

• Mild olive oils are best suited for vinaigrettes on tender green salads or raw vegetables, for mayonnaise and other cold dressings and sauces, for example, in Pesto, Salsa Romesco, and Rouille (see pages 36–37)

• Strong fruity olive oils are ideal for pasta sauces and for marinating fish, meat, vegetables, or cheese. With garlic, the oil forms an aromatic compound. Also, drizzled over cooked vegetables, soups, or casseroles, the flavor of the olive oil is expressed in a masterly fashion. Pizza and focaccia become especially juicy and tasty with olive oil.

• Dishes such as carpaccio or fresh fish become a first class pleasure with a few drops of the finest olive oil.

• Olive oil has proven to be rather stable in hot temperatures. It can easily stand frying temperatures of 350°–375°F. Naturally one does not use the most expensive oil for frying. For frying use an olive oil of the quality grade "virgin olive oil" or "olive oil." It is important that the oil does not reach the smoking point. Caution: For olive oil the point where it develops smoke is lower than with most other oils. If the oil begins to smoke, turn down the heat immediately, and, if necessary, take the pot off the burner briefly

Tips & Tricks

• A quick and delicious meal with olive oil is bruschetta: Rub toasted slices of bread with a clove of garlic that has been cut in half. Drizzle with olive oil, and sprinkle with diced tomatoes and basil strips.

• Meat becomes particularly tender when it is marinated in an olive oil dressing for a few hours prior to roasting or barbecuing.

• Have you bought too much Parmesan? In a closed container, a glass jar is best, cover the cheese with olive oil. It will stay fresh for months in the refrigerator and not dry out. The oil can later be used in pasta, or for drizzling on pizza.

• Put 1 tbs olive oil into the water when boiling pasta. This way pasta won't stick together after cooking.

Bruschetta is great during the summer months, as an hors d'ouevre, or as a snack with a glass of red wine.

Neutral Oils

Oils from sunflower seeds, corn kernels, soybeans, and rape seeds are genuine all-round oils. The taste is mostly neutral, and blends in with all dishes. A special trademark of these oils is their usefulness for cooking. Important for cooking: Pour the oil into a preheated pan. Never heat the oil so much that it smokes. Do not add cold oil while cooking.

Sunflower Oil

For the Indians of North America, the sunflower was already a valued and much used cultivated plant. Today, most of these yellow flowers are grown in the former Soviet Republics (today's Russian Federation), and in the United States. Germany and France are also growing a significant number of sunflowers. The oil that is obtained from the ripe seeds is light yellow, and it has a high content of polyunsaturated fatty acids and vitamin E. Sunflower oil is, for the most part, available as refined oil. Whole food and health food stores offer cold pressed and unrefined sunflower oil as well. The sunflower oil is particularly nutritious if the seeds come from ecologically controlled farms.

Flavor
Cold pressed sunflower oil is distinguished by a fruity flavor typical of its species, which sometimes has a slightly nutty component. Refined sunflower oil tastes neutral.

Use
Cold pressed sunflower oil is preferable for cold cuisine. It is suitable for all green and vegetable salads, for raw vegetables, and for drizzling on cooked vegetables. Refined sunflower oil works well for heating, and especially for crisp browning.

Storing
Cold pressed oil keeps for 12 months, and refined oil keeps for 18 months.

Corn Oil

Corn is one of the ancient cultivated plants. It has been cultivated for about 3000 years. Today it thrives in North America, India, and South Africa. There are two uses for the corn kernel: It contains a lot of starch, the basis for starch flours, and the seed contains a lot of oil. This oil is obtained through careful pressing of soaked and chopped kernels, or with the aid of solvents through extraction. The carefully pressed oil is valued as more healthy. One can choose between two variations: Gently pressed and refined, or gently pressed and unrefined. This is a matter of taste, for both are rich in polyunsaturated fatty acids and vitamin E.

Flavor
The golden yellow unrefined corn oil has a lightly pithy taste. The refined light yellow variety tastes neutral.

Use
Unrefined corn oil is a nice complement to grain dishes and with vegetable salads, perhaps with zucchini or eggplant. As even unrefined corn oil is fairly stable when heated, it is suitable for stir-frying. Refined corn oil is used universally for cold and warm dishes: For raw vegetables, green and vegetable salads, and for mayonnaise. In addition, it is suitable for baking, for instance in Mini Flat Cakes with Herb Oil (see page 55).

Sunflowers are among the most important oil suppliers from plant sources.

The oil obtained from corn kernels has various uses.

Storing
Cold pressed, unrefined oil keeps for 10–12 months, and refined oil keeps for more than 18 months.

Soy Oil

The most important oil plant in the world is called soy. Like all legumes it belongs to the family of Leguminosae, and is grown today primarily in the United States and Asia. The beans contain highly nutritious protein and healthy fat. The fat is usually obtained through hot pressing and refining, as with light yellow oil. Cold pressed, unrefined soy oil is rare. Soy oil contains more than 60 percent polyunsaturated fatty acids.

Flavor
The refined oil tastes neutral; the unrefined tastes slightly bitter.

Use
Suitable for warm and cold cuisine: For sautéing, braising, baking, and roasting, as well as for salads and dips. The oil is very popular in Asian dishes.

Storage
Soy oil keeps for 12 months.

Rapeseed Oil

They characterize the entire landscape, the yellow blooming rape plants—in Europe they are the most commonly cultivated oil seed. Yet the oil is not too well known, and for a long time had a bad reputation on account of its bitter, raspy taste. The reason for that was the high content of eruca acid in the small black seeds. Meanwhile, new types of the cruciferous plants are being cultivated: They deliver oils with a mild, fresh flavor. The fatty acids they contain are largely monounsaturated. The percentage of carotene, the preliminary stage of vitamin A, and vitamin E, is high.

Rapeseed oil is mostly available refined.

Flavor
Refined rapeseed oil tastes neutral; and unrefined is very nutty.

Use
Suitable for warm and cold cuisine, use on all green and vegetable salads, and for vegetable and meat dishes.

Storage
Refined rapeseed oil keeps for 18 months, and unrefined keeps for 6 months.

Flowering rape plant is unmistakable with its yellow blossoms.

Germ, Seed, and Kernal Oils

Wheat Germ Oil

Wheat is much more than the basis for our daily bread. Within the germ of the grain kernel hides a valuable oil. To obtain the oil, the wheat germ is separated from the rest of the grain kernel and then pressed. It is always cold pressed. The gentle golden yellow oil has many superlative benefits: No other oil contains as much vitamin E—more than 200 mg per $\frac{1}{2}$ cup of oil! Also high is the content of polyunsaturated fatty acids.

Flavor
Wheat germ oil tastes slightly like grain.

Use
Preferably used for cold cuisine like raw vegetables, green and vegetable salads, and salads with wild greens and herbs. Vegetable juices are even healthier with a few drops of wheat germ oil.

Storage
Wheat germ oil keeps for eight months. Store opened oil well sealed and in the refrigerator. Ideally, it should be used within two months.

Safflower Oil

It is the oil of the safflower, also called false saffron—a close relative of the sunflower. As with the sunflower, the oil is obtained from the seed kernels. Its special quality: It contains more then 75 percent polyunsaturated fatty acids. That is an absolutely top value; no other oil has such a high content. In addition, the oil is a rich source of vitamin E, 75 mg per $\frac{1}{2}$ cup. Safflower oil is available cold pressed and steam treated, but can also be found refined. Through the steam treatment the taste of the oil is improved and it keeps better.

Flavor
Cold pressed safflower oil has a unique flavor, and as a refined oil, it tastes neutral.

Use
This oil is best used on salads and raw vegetables. Do not heat safflower oil at a high temperature.

Storage
Safflower oil keeps for 12 months.

Linseed Oil

Originally linen, also called flax, was cultivated for the production of linen fabrics. But the seed of the gentle blue flowering plant also contains a highly nutritious oil. It is always obtained through cold pressing. The dark golden yellow, almost amber colored linseed oil had been all but forgotten for a long period of time. But now it can be purchased in health food and whole food stores, and occasionally even in

Wheat is not only an important bread grain, but its oil is also highly nutritious and obtained from its germ.

supermarkets. Linseed oil is particularly rich in triple unsaturated linoleic acid.

Flavor
Linseed oil tastes very intense and slightly bitter.

Use
Thanks to its distinctive, dominant taste, linseed oil goes well with only a few dishes. It is suitable exclusively for cold cuisine. When heated, harmful substances develop. It is best known for the Silesian dish "Potatoes boiled in their jackets with linseed oil quark" (see Tip below).

Storage
Linseed oil keeps for six months, but always keep it refrigerated! Use fairly soon after opening.

TIP!
Linseed Oil Quark
Mix 1 lb nonfat quark or farmer's cheese with 2 tbs linseed oil, and stir until creamy. Season with salt and pepper. Sprinkle with chives. Serve with potatoes boiled in their jackets.

Pumpkinseed Oil

The seeds of different kinds of pumpkins, the oil pumpkins, are an extraordinary source for oil. It entices the user through its interesting look: Pumpkinseed oil shimmers dark green. The oil is obtained by cold pressing the previously roasted seeds, and has a healthy fatty acid pattern. More than 50 percent of the fatty acids are polyunsaturated. The oil is a favorite among gourmets, and is a specialty of Syria.

Flavor
Pumpkinseed oil is distinguished through a strong nutty and spicy flavor.

Use
Suitable for dressings on hefty salads like sausage, meat, potato, egg, or cabbage salad. Dishes with vegetables, legumes, or soups should be sprinkled with the oil only after cooking.

Storage
Pumpkinseed oil keeps for 12 months.

Grapeseed Oil

The seeds of grapes are the basis of this gourmet oil. The French were the first to have the idea to press the seeds. The result: A light, slightly greenish oil with plenty of polyunsaturated fatty acids and vitamin E, as well as procyanidin, which is considered good for cancer protection. Grapeseed oil can be cold pressed, unrefined and greenish in color, or obtained through extraction in which case it is refined and colorless.

Flavor
Cold pressed unrefined oil tastes fruity and nutty, refined oil is neutral.

Use
Suited for cold and warm cuisine. The flavor of the oil stays discretely in the background. Very good on salads with poultry, and fish, or on green salads and fruit salads. The oil is recommended for fondues and for short frying.

Storage
The oil keeps for 15 months.

Farmer's wife in Syria with seeds from an oil pumpkin.

Nut Oils

Nuts are not only for nibbling. From nuts you can extract delicious oils. From peanut oil to the rare pistachio oil, they are all rich in flavor.

Peanut Oil

It is among the most important oil. The peanut kernels are usually ground, warm-pressed, and then refined. The light yellow oil is rich in monounsaturated fatty acids.

Flavor
Peanut oil tastes neutral.

Use
Peanut oil can be heated to high temperatures. It is ideal for roasting, barbecuing, and deep-frying. It is very popular in Asian cuisine. In cold cuisine it goes well whenever the unique flavor of another oil or other ingredients and spice need a neutral support. For instance, try it in mayonnaise and herb dressings.

Storage
You can store peanut oil for up to 18 months. When refrigerated, the oil starts to thicken. Brought to room temperature, it becomes fluid and clear again.

Sesame Oil

Sesame oil comes mostly from Africa or Asia. The oil produced from roasted sesame seeds tastes especially aromatic; it is recognizable by its intense aroma and its amber color. Normally the color of sesame oil is light yellow. The amount of mono- and polyunsaturated fatty acids is about equal.

Flavor
Sesame oil tastes intensely spicy and nutty.

Use
The amber colored sesame oil is a typical spice oil. It gives salads, sauces, and meat dishes from the Orient and wok dishes from the Far East a distinctively strong flavor. This oil is drizzled sparingly over cooked dishes. The light yellow sesame oil can be heated, and it gives the Japanese fondue specialty, tempura, its characteristic flavors.

Storage
Sesame oil keeps for 18 months.

Walnut Oil

The delicate aroma of the light clear oil is a favorite in the gourmet's kitchen. It is pressed from fresh nuts, and usually remains unrefined. Walnut oil often comes from France. The amount of polyunsaturated fatty acids is above 70 percent.

Flavor
The oil has a delicate walnut flavor.

Use
Ideal for raw vegetables, marinated vegetables such as beets, and green salads, especially oak leaf, lamb's lettuce, and endive. Legume salads are enhanced through the use of walnut oil.

Storage
You can store this oil for up to 12 months. In contact with air, walnut oil oxidizes particularly fast. Close the container tightly, immediately after use, and store in a cool place!

Nuts are the basis for valuable oils: Hazelnuts, walnuts, almonds, peanuts, pistachios, and sesame (from left to right).

Hazelnut, Almond, and Pistachio Oil

These oils are rarities, and are usually only available in specialty food markets. They are cold pressed and very healthy.

Flavor
The taste of the oil depends on the type of nut used in the oil.

Use
For desserts and fruit salads, spooned in drops, and never to be heated.

Storage
Nut oils keep for six months. Keep them cool and use quickly after opening the container.

Aromatized Oils

Aroma oils can be made at home without much effort (see pages 34–35). The choices of aromatized oil specialties that you can purchase are always changing. The oils are usually made from olive oil or sunflower oil. Herbs such as basil, rosemary, bay leaf, and garlic add wonderful aromas and can be beautifully displayed in bottles of oil. With these oils, pizza, noodles, and salads get that extra something. Chili oil gives the appropriate sharpness—ideal for Mexican dishes. Barbecue oils are especially stabile at high temperatures, and add color and the desired flavor. Special pearls among the aromatized oils are truffle and porcini oils. They create an extraordinarily concentrated taste experience, and drop by little drop they season risotto, carpaccio, pasta, or salads. They can even turn potato soup into a culinary treat.

Special Oils

Special oils are usually made from different kinds of oils. They have to serve various functions. Diet oils are specifically designed for people with high cholesterol levels, and are usually enriched with vitamin A, D, and E. Other oil mixtures like the so-called multi-fruit oils are used for cold cuisine. And where the kitchen is hot, there are special oils available that can be heated well: Wok oil, fondue oil, deep-frying oil, and plant oils with butter tastes.

Average Fat Composition of Oils

	Saturated	Monounsaturated	Polyunsaturated	Vitamin E
Safflower oil	10.0	11.8	75.0	75.0
Linseed oil	9.6	17.2	72.0	2.0
Corn oil	13.4	31.6	50.9	30.0
Olive oil	13.6	73.2	9.0	12.0
Rapeseed oil	5.7	68.5	27.7	15.3
Sesame oil	12.9	40.1	42.5	4.1
Soy oil	13.9	20.6	61.0	15.0
Sunflower oil	11.5	22.4	60.7	55.0
Grapeseed oil	8.9	16.7	66.0	32.0
Walnut oil	8.6	15.7	70.9	3.2
Wheat germ oil	17.2	15.6	64.7	215

Fatty acids measured in g per 1/2 cup oil. Vitamin E measured in mg per 100 g of oil.

Homemade Spice Oils

Take herbs and garlic, let them settle in the oil for a while, and you have spice oil. Store in a cool, dark place. It should keep for approximately 6 months.

Herb Oil

4 sprigs fresh herbs (e.g. rosemary, thyme, basil, oregano, mint)
2 cups extra virgin olive oil

1 Wash herbs and shake dry. Carefully pat dry. Ideally dry overnight. The herbs must be completely dry.

2 Place the herbs in a bottle with oil. They must be completely covered with oil. Allow to stand at room temperature for 3 weeks. Then pour the oil through a strainer. Remove the herbs.

Use
• for barbecue marinades
• for salad dressings use on green or vegetable salads, and for raw vegetables
• for pasta sauces
• for pizza

VARIATIONS

You can take only one kind of herb and use it to make rosemary oil, basil oil, mint oil, etc. Quite nice are also herb mixtures, for example, rosemary, lavender, thyme, and oregano to create a "Provence oil."

Garlic Oil

8 cloves garlic
2 cups extra virgin olive oil

1 Peel garlic cloves and add to the oil in a bottle. Allow to stand for at least 3 weeks and store at room temperature.

2 Then the oil is ready to use. The garlic cloves can stay in the oil, or they can be taken out and used like fresh cloves of garlic.

Use
• for garlic croutons
• for vinaigrettes, for example with green salads
• for marinating vegetables
• for garlic mayonnaise

Ginger–Sweet Lime Oil

1 organic sweet lime
2¹/₂ inch piece fresh ginger
1 cup soy oil

1 Wash sweet lime and dry. Cut off the peel in spiral form. Peel ginger and slice it.

2 Place sweet lime peel and ginger into a bottle with oil. Allow to stand at room temperature for at least 2 weeks. Sweet lime peel and ginger can stay in the oil and be used as seasoning.

Use
• for vinaigrettes use over green salads, for example with iceberg , chicory, or Chinese cabbage
• for seasoning Asian rice dishes or wok vegetables
• for marinating fish or poultry.

Chili Oil

6 red chile peppers
1¹/₃ cups peanut or soy oil

1 Wash and dry chile peppers. Remove the stems, cut the pods in half lengthwise, remove the seeds, and slice into pieces ¹/₂ inch long.

2 Lightly heat the oil in a pot; do not let it smoke. Turn off heat, add chiles, and let them stand until the oil is cooled. Transfer the oil and chiles into a bottle.

3 The chile strips can stay in the oil, and can be chopped and used. If preferred, pour the oil through a strainer.

Use
• for steaming and seasoning Asian vegetable dishes
• for chile con carne
• for spicy barbecue marinades
• for pasta
• for Rouille (see page 37)

Porcini Mushroom Oil

1 oz dried porcini mushrooms
1¹/₃ cups sunflower or corn oil

1 Place mushrooms in a wide-rimmed jar. Pour in the oil and close tightly.

2 Allow the mushrooms to stand at room temperature in the oil for 3 weeks. Then pour the oil with the mushrooms through filter paper.

Use
• for vinaigrettes, for example, with oak leaf or arugula
• for drizzling on a baked potato
• for seasoning risotto and mushroom sauces
• the mushroom can be used separately: For this, soak the mushrooms in water for 15 minutes, then take them out of the water, and slice into fine pieces. Filter the soaking water. Mushrooms and soaking water can be used to season rice dishes, stews, or gravies.

Clockwise from the top: Ginger-Sweet Lime Oil, Herb Oil, Chili Oil, Porcini Oil, and Garlic Oil

Pesto

- Specialty from Italy
- Fast

Serves 6–8:

3 bunches fresh basil
3 cloves garlic
Salt to taste
Black pepper to taste
3 tbs pine nuts
3 heaping tbs freshly grated Parmesan
3 heaping tbs freshly grated pecorino
8 tbs extra virgin olive oil

Prep time: 20 minutes
Storing time: 3 weeks (refrigerated)

Per serving (8) approx.:
102 calories
2 g protein/10 g fat/2 g carb

1 Wash basil, pat dry with paper towels, and pick the leaves off. Peel garlic and chop coarsely.

2 For preparation in the blender, put basil, garlic, salt, pepper, pine nuts, and cheese together in the blender, while adding oil a little at a time.

3 For preparation in the mortar, first crush the garlic, pine nuts, and salt and pepper in the mortar. Then cut the basil leaves into small pieces, and add to mixture. Crush everything with the pestle. Mix in the cheese. Stir in the oil, a little at a time. Serve as a pasta sauce over fresh fettuccine or other thin noodles.

TIP!

If you want to keep the pesto for a while, put it in a jar with a tight lid, cover it with olive oil, and store the sauce in the refrigerator.

Salsa Romanesco

- Specialty from Spain
- Prepare ahead

Serves 4:

1 red bell pepper
1 tomato
1 red chile pepper
4 tbs shelled almonds
1/2 slice toasted bread
1 clove garlic
Salt to taste
1 tbs sherry vinegar
5 tbs extra virgin olive oil

Prep time: 40 minutes

Per serving approx.: 154 calories
3 g protein/14 g fat/6 g carb

1 Wash bell pepper, cut in half and trim. Roast, skin side up, for 10 minutes, under the broiler, remove, and cover with a damp kitchen towel. Let cool, and remove skin from the bell pepper, and cut in strips.

2 Pour boiling water over the tomato, remove skin and seeds and chop. Wash chile pepper, cut in half, remove seeds, and slice fine. Roast almonds in a pan without grease. Dice the bread. Peel garlic and chop.

3 Purée almonds, diced bread, tomatoes, red pepper, chile pepper, garlic, salt, vinegar, and 1 tbs olive oil in a blender. Little by little, mix in the remaining olive oil. The sauce goes well with barbecued meat and fish, as well as with steamed fresh vegetables.

VARIATION

Improve the salsa at the end by adding 1 tsp almond or pistachio oil.

R E C I P E S

Rouille

- Specialty from France
- Classic

Serves 4:

| 4 cloves garlic |
| 1 small potato (cooked in the jacket) |
| Salt to taste |
| $^1/_2$ tsp cayenne pepper |
| Black pepper to taste |
| 1 large pinch saffron powder |
| $^1/_2$ tsp fresh lemon juice |
| 1 egg yolk |
| $^1/_2$ cup olive oil |

Prep time: 30 minutes

Per serving approx.: 288 calories
1 g protein/30 g fat/5 g
carbohydrate

1 Peel garlic and chop fine. Peel potato and mash with a fork. Crush garlic and salt in a mortar.

2 Mix cayenne, black pepper, saffron, and lemon juice with the garlic. Work the potato into the garlic paste with the pestle. Mix in the egg yolk.

3 Pour oil, a little at a time, into the mixture, emulsifying it in with a whisk. Rouille is served with the famous fish soup, bouillabaisse. Before serving, stir 2–3 tbs of the fish liquid into the sauce to lighten it and enhance the flavor.

TIP!

Instead of olive oil, you can use Chili Oil (see page 34). That makes it quite spicy, so the cayenne pepper can be left out or reduced.

Frankfurt Green Sauce

- Famous recipe
- Sophisticated

Serves 4:

3 tbs chopped fresh herbs (any mixture of parsley, chives, tarragon, dill, borage, chervil, sorrel)
2 shallots
4 tbs white wine vinegar
4 hard-cooked eggs
1/2 cup cream
1/2 cup yogurt from whole milk (not nonfat or low fat)
1 tbs sharp mustard
Salt to taste
White pepper to taste
4 tbs sunflower or corn oil

Prep time: 30 minutes
(plus 1 hour standing time)

Per serving approx.: 275 calories
11 g protein/22 g fat/13 g
carbohydrate

1 Sort and wash herbs, spin dry, and chop very fine. Peel and dice shallots. In a bowl, pour vinegar over the herbs and shallots. Cover, and let rest at room temperature for 30 minutes.

2 Peel eggs and chop fine. Stir together, cream, yogurt and mustard. Season generously with salt and pepper. A little at a time, stirring constantly, and then add the oil. Mix in 3 of the chopped eggs.

3 Whisk together the herb vinegar mixture with the cream sauce. Allow sauce to stand an additional 30 minutes, covered, in the refrigerator. Before serving, stir well and sprinkle with the remaining chopped egg. The sauce goes well with cooked beef, steamed fish, or vegetables like barbecued corn on the cob.

VARIATION

Asian Green Sauce
Place 3 tbs chopped fresh Asian-style herbs (e.g. cilantro, garlic chives, parsley) in a bowl. Wash and trim 2 green onions, and chop fine. Allow herbs and onions to stand in 4 tbs rice vinegar. Follow the rest of the preparation in the above recipe. Instead of sunflower oil use Ginger-Sweet Lime Oil (see page 34). If desired, mix in 1 tbs chopped peanuts. Serve the sauce with barbecued meat or vegetables on skewers.

Sauce Béarnaise

● Classic
● Takes practice

Serves 4:

2 shallots

8 white peppercorns

1 tbs each minced
fresh chervil and
fresh tarragon leaves
(or ³/₄ tsp each dried
chervil and dried
tarragon leaves)

4 tbs white wine vinegar

4 tbs tarragon vinegar
(homemade, see page 16,
or store bought)

3 egg yolks

8 tbs cold butter (1 stick),
cut into pieces

Salt to taste

Prep time: 30 minutes

Per serving approx.: 342 calories
6 g protein/30 g fat/17 g carb

1 Peel shallots and dice
fine. Coarsely crush pep-
percorns in a mortar. Wash
herbs and chop fine.

2 In a small pot, bring
vinegar, shallots, peppercorns, and half of the
herbs to boiling. Gently
simmer, uncovered, until
half the liquid is evapo-
rated, then allow the
mixture to cool.

3 For the rest of the
preparation, you need a
double boiler. Fill a wide
pot half full with water,
and heat it. Then place a
stainless steel bowl with a
round bottom, or a small
pot over the hot water.

4 Place the egg yolks
in the small pot of the
double boiler. Add the
vinegar liquid, pouring it
through a strainer, and
add salt. Beat the egg
yolk mixture with a whisk,
until the egg yolk becomes
foamy and creamy. Then,
a few pieces at a time,
stir in the butter. The
sauce must never boil or
it will curdle. Mix the
remaining herbs into the
sauce, and season with
additional salt, if needed.
Serve at once. The sauce
goes well with asparagus,
steaks, light steamed
meat, or fish.

VARIATION

Orange-Béarnaise
Instead of the tarragon
vinegar, use Orange Vinegar
(see page 17), and instead
of tarragon and chervil, use
parsley. This sauce goes
beautifully with artichokes.

Classic Vinaigrette

● Fast
● Prepare ahead

Serves 4:

Salt to taste
White pepper to taste
$^1/_4$ tsp mustard
2 tbs white wine vinegar
5 tbs olive oil
1 tbs chopped fresh herbs
(e.g. chives, parsley,
chervil, dill)

Prep time: 10 minutes

Per serving approx.: 82 calories
0 g protein/9 g fat/0 g
carbohydrate

1 Whisk together salt, pepper, mustard, and vinegar.

2 Add the oil, and whisk until the dressing is well mixed. Mix in the herbs, and season to taste with salt and pepper. Vinaigrette goes with green salads, tomato and cucumber salad, and bean and potato salad, and artichokes and asparagus. It is also suitable for marinating meat, or fish.

VARIATION

Improve the vinaigrette by adding 1 tbs balsamic vinegar.

Sherry Vinaigrette

● Sophisticated
● Easy

Serves 4:

Salt to taste
Black pepper to taste
1 tbs sherry vinegar
1 tsp balsamic vinegar
1 tbs freshly squeezed
orange juice
2 tbs grapeseed oil
2 tbs walnut oil

Prep time: 10 minutes

Per serving approx.: 68 calories
0 g protein/7 g fat/1 g
carbohydrate

1 Whisk together salt, pepper, vinegar, and orange juice, until the salt dissolves.

2 Whisk in both kinds of oil, and season the vinaigrette to taste. The sherry vinaigrette goes especially well with green salads like radicchio or arugula, and with salad compositions that include artichokes, chicory, or pale celery.

VARIATION

Instead of orange juice, use Orange Vinegar (see page 17), it works well in this dressing.

Dill Honey Dressing

● Fast
● Easy

Serves 4:

1 hard-cooked egg
1 tbs mustard
Salt to taste
Black pepper to taste
2 tbs honey vinegar
4 tbs safflower oil
$^1/_2$ bunch fresh dill

Prep time: 10 minutes

Per serving approx.: 86 calories
2 g protein/ 9 g fat/ 1 g
carbohydrate

1 Peel the egg and chop it fine. Mix mustard, salt, pepper, and vinegar until smooth. Stir in the oil.

2 Wash the dill and cut fine. Mix in the dill and the chopped egg, and season to taste with salt and pepper. The dill honey dressing goes well with salads topped with smoked fish, and with cucumber salad and green salads.

VARIATION

Instead of safflower oil, use 2 tbs each of wheat germ oil and sunflower oil. Goes perfectly with grain salads.

Mayonnaise

● Takes a bit of time
● Classic

Serves 4-6:

2 fresh egg yolks
$^1/_4$ tsp salt
White pepper to taste
1 tbs white wine vinegar
or lemon juice
$^2/_3$ cup corn, sunflower,
soy or rapeseed oil

Prep time: 10 minutes
Storing time: 1 week
(refrigerated)

Per serving approx.: 129 calories
1 g protein/14 g fat/0 g
carbohydrate

1 Whisk together egg yolks, salt, pepper, and vinegar, using a wire whisk or the whisk attachment of an electric hand beater.

2 Stir in the oil, at first in drops, then in a thin stream, so that a smooth sauce is created. Mayonnaise is ideal for salads with noodles, fish, seafood, potatoes, poultry, artichokes, chicory, celery, or cauliflower.

TIP!

Mayonnaise may also be prepared in a blender or food processor, following the above instructions.

VARIATIONS

Light mayonnaise

If the classic mayonnaise is too rich for you, you can make it lighter: Mix only half the basic recipe, and stir in 3 tbs yogurt.

Herb mayonnaise

Mix 3 tbs finely chopped herbs into the completed mayonnaise. Parsley, chervil, chives, and tarragon work very well.

Garlic mayonnaise

Press 2 peeled garlic cloves through a garlic press, and mix into the completed mayonnaise.

Thousand Island Dressing

Mix in ½ red bell pepper, diced fine, 1 small, finely chopped pickled gherkin, 3 tbs tomato ketchup, ½ tsp sweet paprika, and 1 large pinch cayenne pepper.

In the photo from top to bottom: Mayonnaise, Sherry Vinaigrette, Classic Vinaigrette, and Dill Honey Dressing.

Carrots with Sesame Oil

● Sophisticated
● Easy

Serves 4:

1 1/2 lb carrots
1/2 cup vegetable broth
2 green onions
1/2 clove garlic
4 tbs fruit vinegar
Salt to taste
White pepper to taste
1/4 tsp sesame seeds
1/2 tsp honey
1 tbs sesame oil
4 tbs soy oil
1 bunch fresh chives
1/4 cup cashew nuts

Prep time: 30 minutes
Marinating time: 1 day

Per serving approx.: 263 calories
5 g protein/16 g fat/28 g
carbohydrates

1 Wash carrots, peel, and slice. Bring vegetable broth to boiling. Add the carrots, and simmer for 7 minutes until al dente.

2 Trim and wash green onions, and slice fine. Peel garlic and dice very fine. Whisk together vinegar with salt, pepper, sesame seeds, and honey. Stir in oils and garlic.

3 Mix carrots and vegetable broth, while still warm, with the marinade and green onions. Allow vegetables to marinate in the refrigerator, covered, for 1 day.

4 Wash chives, and chop fine. Arrange the carrots with the marinade on a platter. Sprinkle with chives and cashew nuts. The carrots are great served as a delicate vegetarian hors d'oeuvre, or as a side dish with spicy stir-fried strips of meat.

VARIATION

Fans of Asian cuisine use rice vinegar for the marinade, and replace the chives with garlic chives. The carrots are especially attractive, when they are garnished with the white, star-shaped flowers of the garlic chives. The flowers can be eaten too—they taste slightly sweet.

Beets with Walnuts

● Specialty from France
● For a cold buffet

Serves 4:

1¼ lb beets
Salt to taste
Black pepper to taste
2 tbs raspberry vinegar
2 tbs red wine vinegar
1 pinch sugar
1 pinch ground allspice
2 tbs walnut oil
2 tbs corn oil
2 shallots
¼ cup walnuts
1 bunch fresh
Italian parsley

Prep time: 30 minutes
Cooking time: 1 hour

Per serving approx.: 178 calories
6 g protein/10 g fat/21 g
carbohydrates

1 Wash beets, put in a pot, barely cover with water, and add salt. Simmer the vegetables, covered, over medium heat, for 1 hour.

2 For the marinade, whisk together salt, pepper, vinegar, sugar, and allspice, as well as the 2 oils.

3 Drain beets in a strainer, and rinse with cold water. Peel the beets and cut in half. Cut in slices about ½ inch thick, either with a regular knife, or with a crinkle cutter.

4 Carefully, mix the still warm vegetable slices with the marinade. Marinate at least 2 hours, or better, overnight.

5 Peel shallots and dice. Coarsely chop nuts. Wash parsley and cut fine. Mix the beets with the shallots before serving. Sprinkle with nuts and parsley. The beets taste good as an hors d'oeuvre with a slice of whole-grain bread. As a sweet-sour side dish, it goes well with cooked beef.

VARIATION

Beets and Apple
Wash, peel, quarter, and remove seeds from a small apple. Slice it, and mix with the beet slices. Instead of walnut oil, hazelnut oil also tastes very good.

Marinated Peppers

● Low calorie
● Prepare ahead

Serves 4:

2 red and 2 yellow
bell peppers each
1 clove garlic
1 tbs lemon vinegar
3 tbs sunflower oil
Salt to taste
Black pepper to taste

Prep time: 30 minutes
Marinating time: 5 hours
Storing time: 1 week
(refrigerated)

Per serving approx.: 67 calories
1 g protein/6 g fat/4 g
carbohydrates

1 Wash bell peppers, cut in half, and trim. Roast, skin side up, under the broiler for 10 minutes until the skin blisters. If you don't have a broiler, roast them in a preheated oven at 500°F on the top rack.

2 Let the bell peppers cool, covered, with a damp kitchen towel. Peel garlic and chop fine. Stir together vinegar, oil and garlic, and season with salt and pepper.

3 Skin the bell peppers, and place them on a platter, dribble with the marinade. Let them marinate, covered, in the refrigerator for 5 hours.

Eggplant in Rosemary Oil

● Sophisticated
● Easy

Serves 4:

Salt to taste
1½ lb eggplant
2 cloves garlic
1 bunch fresh basil
Black pepper to taste
4 tbs white wine vinegar
4 tbs herb oil with
rosemary (see page 34)

Prep time: 20 minutes
Marinating time: 1 hour
Storing time: 3 days
(refrigerated)

Per serving approx.: 98 calories
1 g protein/7 g fat/9 g
carbohydrates

1 Bring a pot of salted water to boiling. Trim and wash eggplants, cut in ½ inch cubes, and cook them in boiling water for 5 minutes. Drain.

2 Peel garlic and chop fine. Wash basil and cut half of it in strips, and reserve other half for garnish. Stir together salt, pepper, garlic, and vinegar.

3 Mix the warm eggplants with the marinade, and the basil strips. Marinate for 1 hour and then mix in the oil, and garnish with the remaining basil.

Thyme Mushrooms

● For guests
● Easy

Serves 4:

3 green onions
1 small clove garlic
3 sprigs fresh thyme,
or 1 tsp dried thyme
½ cup vegetable broth
6 tbs dry white wine or
vegetable broth
1 tbs shallot vinegar
(homemade, see page 16
or store bought)
Salt to taste
Black pepper to taste
1 lb small brown
mushrooms (e.g. crimini)
4 tbs extra virgin olive oil

Prep time: 30 minutes
Marinating time: 2 hours
Storing: 2 days (refrigerated)

Per serving approx.: 152 calories
4 g protein/8 g fat/14 g
carbohydrates

1 Trim and wash green onions, and cut into bite-sized pieces. Peel garlic and slice fine. Wash thyme and strip off the leaves.

2 Bring the broth, wine, and vinegar to boiling in a pot. Add garlic and thyme, and season generously with salt and pepper, cover, and simmer at medium heat for 15 minutes. Clean and trim the mushrooms.

3 Turn the burner off, but leave the pot on the burner, and put the mushrooms into the hot liquid for 4 minutes. Add the onions, and let them stand for 1 more minute. Allow the mushrooms to cool off in the liquid. Put mushrooms with the liquid in a bowl. Pour oil on top, cover, and allow to stand in the refrigerator for 2 hours. Garnish with additional thyme, if desired.

VARIATIONS

Instead of shallot vinegar, another excellent harmonic complement to the mushrooms is garlic or bay leaf vinegar. Another nice addition to the mushrooms, is a dribble of truffle vinegar at the end.

**In the picture top:
Eggplant in Rosemary Oil
In the picture in the
middle: Thyme Mushrooms
In the picture bottom:
Marinated Peppers**

Spicy Cauliflower and Broccoli

● Exotic
● Sharp

**Makes 3 jars
(3 cups each):**

1¹/₂ lb cauliflower
³/₄ lb broccoli
1 tbs salt
¹/₄ lb shallots
4 red chile peppers
2 stalks lemon grass
3¹/₂ cups lemon vinegar
(homemade, see page 17
or store bought)
¹/₂ cup sugar
2 bay leaves

Prep time: 30 minutes
Storing time: 2 months

Per serving approx.: 266 calories
7 g protein/1 g fat/70 g carb

1 Wash cauliflower and broccoli, and separate into rosettes. Peel broccoli stems. Heat 4 quarts salted water. Cook the vegetables in boiling water for 5 minutes, and drain in a colander set over a bowl, saving the cooking liquid. Immediately immerse the vegetables in ice water.

2 Peel shallots and quarter. Wash peppers, cut in half lengthwise, and remove the seeds. Wash lemon grass, remove tough outer leaves, and cut into pieces 1¹/₂ inches long.

3 Simmer vinegar, 3 cups of the vegetable cooking liquid, sugar, shallots, chile peppers, lemon grass, and bay leaf, covered, for 5 minutes. Add vegetables, and bring to a boil once more, briefly. Pour into jars and close. Serve with rice dishes.

Mustard Pickles with Borage

● Inexpensive
● Easy

**Makes 2 jars
(3 cups each):**

2 lb yellow
canning cucumbers
4 tsp salt
4 borage leaves
1²/₃ cups herb vinegar with
dill (homemade, see page
16 or store bought)
¹/₂ cup sugar
1 bay leaf
2 tbs mustard seeds
1 tbs allspice corns
2 cloves
1 tbs white peppercorns

Prep time: 25 minutes
Resting time: 12 hours
Storing: 3 months
(in a cool place)

Per serving approx.: 342 calories
6 g protein/4 g fat/80 g
carbohydrates

1 Peel cucumbers, cut in half lengthwise, remove seeds, and slice ¹/₂ inch thick. Put cucumbers in a bowl, sprinkle with salt, and let stand overnight.

2 Drain cucumbers in a colander. Wash borage, dry with paper towels, and cut in strips.

3 In a pot, bring vinegar, 1²/₃ cups water, sugar, and the spices to boiling. Simmer cucumbers and borage for 1 minute in the liquid. Transfer cucumbers and their liquid into jars, and close at once. The cucumbers go with open-faced ham sandwiches, or cold cuts and cheese.

Pumpkin in Orange Vinegar

● Sweet-sour
● Easy

**Makes 2 jars
(1²/₃ cups each):**

1¹/₂ lb small pumpkin
(or other winter squash)
1¹/₂ inch slice fresh ginger
¹/₂ cup orange vinegar
(see page 17)
1¹/₄ cups sugar
1 cinnamon stick
Peel of half organic
orange, cut in a spiral

Prep time: 30 minutes
Marinating time: 12 hours
Storing: 4 months
(in a cool place)

Per serving approx.: 587 calories
3 g protein/1 g fat/153 g
carbohydrates

1 Peel pumpkin, cut in half, and remove the seeds. Cut pumpkin into large cubes. Peel ginger and slice. Bring vinegar, ¹/₂ cup water, sugar, cinnamon stick, ginger and orange peel to a boil, and then turn off.

2 Put pumpkin pieces into the hot vinegar liquid. Cover, and allow to stand overnight in a cool place. Then bring pumpkin and liquid to a boil, and simmer over medium heat for 8 minutes.

3 Lift the pumpkin cubes out with a skimmer and place into jars. Simmer the liquid for 5 minutes in the open pot, then pour it over the pumpkin. Close jars immediately. Serve the pumpkin as a side dish with meat, game, and cheese on toast.

Shallots in Red Wine Vinegar

● For guests
● Sophisticated

**Makes 2 jars
(1²/₃ cups each):**

³/₄ lb small shallots
Salt to taste
8 tbs red wine vinegar
1 tbs honey
3 tbs rapeseed or
sunflower oil
2 tbs sugar
Black pepper to taste

Prep time: 45 minutes
Storing: 3 months
(in a cool place)

Per serving approx.: 306 calories
4 g protein/11 g fat/52 g
carbohydrates

1 Peel the shallots. Bring 3¹/₂ cups salted water to a boil. Simmer shallots for 5 minutes, then pour through a colander set over a bowl, saving the cooking liquid. Slightly heat the vinegar in a pot and dissolve the honey in the pot.

2 Heat oil in a saucepan. Fry and stir shallots for 3 minutes on medium heat. Sprinkle with sugar, and season with salt and pepper.

3 Pour honey vinegar over the shallots. Cook shallots for 5 minutes, uncovered, stirring occasionally. Add ¹/₂ cup cooking liquid and bring to a brief boil. Transfer shallots and liquid into jars, and close jars at once. The shallots go well with raw ham and crunchy bread as an hors d'oeuvre, but also as a side dish with stir-fried or barbecued meat.

Feta Cheese Skewers

● Easy
● Sophisticated

Serves 4:

1 lb feta cheese
2 sprigs fresh rosemary
4 cloves garlic
4 chile peppers
1 1/2 cups extra virgin
olive oil
6 oz black and
green pitted olives
(3 oz of each olive)
4 shish kebab skewers,
or 4 rosemary stems,
needles removed

Prep time: 30 minutes
Marinating time: 2–3 days
(in a cool place)

Per serving approx.: 395 calories
15 g protein/33 g fat/11 g
carbohydrates

1 Cut cheese into bite-sized cubes. Wash rosemary stems and dry. Peel garlic, cut chile peppers in half, and remove seeds.

2 Put all ingredients in a jar. Pour oil over them and allow to marinate for 2–3 days.

3 Alternate putting cheese and olives on skewers or rosemary stems.

VARIATION

Instead of garlic cloves, use Garlic Oil (see page 34).

Marinated Goat Cheese

● Fast
● For guests

Serves 4:

8 leaves oak leaf lettuce
1 bunch fresh chives
8 small goat cheeses
(about 1 1/2 oz each)
Black pepper to taste
Salt to taste
3 tbs sherry vinegar
4 tbs pumpkin seed oil

Prep time: 15 minutes

Per serving approx.: 449 calories
26 g protein/36 g fat/6 g
carbohydrates

1 Wash lettuce and chives, and shake dry. Slice half of the chives fine.

2 Arrange lettuce leaves and cheeses on plates. Sprinkle coarsely ground pepper on the cheese. Stir 1 pinch of salt into the vinegar. Whisk in the oil. Mix the sliced chives into the vinaigrette.

3 Dribble the marinade over the cheese and lettuce leaves, and garnish with the remaining chives. The goat cheese makes a delicate hors d'oeuvre served with whole-grain rolls.

Stuffed Mozzarella

● Easy
● Sophisticated

Serves 4:

4 fresh mozzarella balls
1/2 red bell pepper
8 pimiento-stuffed
green olives
1 shallot
12 small fresh sage leaves
2 tbs balsamic vinegar
4 tbs extra virgin olive oil
Salt to taste
Black pepper to taste

Prep time: 25 minutes

Per serving approx.: 490 calories
28 g protein/39 g fat/7 g
carbohydrates

1 Drain mozzarella and cut in half crosswise. From the middle of each half, remove about 2 tsp of cheese and dice fine. Wash and trim the bell pepper, and dice it small. Slice the olives fine. Peel shallot and dice fine. Wash sage leaves.

2 Drizzle balsamic vinegar and olive oil over the olives and bell pepper. Mix in the diced cheese and shallots. Season with salt and pepper.

3 Stuff the cheese halves. Garnish with any of the remaining filling and sage leaves.

Mozzarella Tomatoes in Basil

● For a cold buffet
● Prepare ahead

Serves 4:

8 oz cherry tomatoes
1 bunch fresh basil
8 oz fresh mini
mozzarella balls
1 tbs preserved green
peppercorns
1 1/3 cups extra virgin
olive oil

Prep time: 15 minutes
Marinating time: 3–4 days
(in a cool place)

Per serving approx.: 275 calories
14 g protein/22 g fat/5 g
carbohydrates

1 Wash tomatoes and dry. Wash basil and pat dry with paper towels. Drain cheese balls, and poke them with a fork several times. Rinse peppercorns and pat dry.

2 Layer all ingredients in a jar. Pour oil over them, so that everything is covered. Allow to marinate for 3–4 days.

Clockwise from left top: Feta Cheese Skewers, Marinated Goat Cheese, Mozzarella Tomatoes in Basil, and Stuffed Mozzarella

Trout and Vegetables in White Wine Vinegar

● Prepare ahead
● Sophisticated

Serves 4:

4 cleaned and prepared trout (¹/₂ lb each)
Salt to taste
Black pepper to taste
1 tbs flour
²/₃ cup sunflower oil
2 onions
1 carrot
1 stalk leek
1 clove garlic
10 white peppercorns
1 cup white wine vinegar
1 cup dry white wine (e.g. Riesling, or vegetable broth)
1 cup vegetable broth
8 whole allspice
2 sprigs fresh rosemary
2 sprigs fresh thyme
1 pinch sugar
1 bunch fresh dill

Prep time: 40 minutes
Marinating time: 3 days
(in a cool place)

Per serving approx.: 574 calories
57 g protein/21 g fat/30 g carb

1 Wash the fish under cold running water, then pat dry. Sprinkle fish, inside and out with salt and pepper. Dust outside of fish with flour. Heat all but 2 tbs of the oil in an oval pan. Fry the trout in the pan for 5 minutes on each side. Place the trout in a serving dish large enough to hold the trout and the marinade. Allow to cool.

2 Peel onions, and dice. Peel carrot and slice. Trim leek and wash, and cut in fine strips. Peel garlic. Heat the remaining 2 tbs of oil. Briefly fry onions, carrots and leeks in the oil. Add vinegar, wine, and broth. Add garlic, peppercorns, allspice, herbs, salt, pepper, and sugar. Bring the liquid to boiling once more, and then simmer at a lower temperature for 5 minutes.

3 Cover the fish with the lukewarm liquid. Allow to stand, covered, in the refrigerator for 3 days. Just before serving, wash the dill, and chop fine. At serving time, sprinkle dill over trout. Preserved trout are great for brunch, or for a hefty buffet or picnic. Goes well with a hearty, whole-grain bread.

Note: As the trout marinates for 3 days, before serving and garnishing with fresh dill, you may wish to purchase the dill on the day you serve the fish.

TIP!

Is the frying pan too small for four trout, fry the fish in two portions, two at a time.

Young Herring (Matjes) in Red Wine Vinegar

● Classic from Scandinavia
● For a cold buffet

Serves 6–8:

³/₄ lb red onions
1 cup red wine vinegar
1 cup dry white wine or vegetable broth
¹/₂ cup sugar
2 bay leaves
2 cloves
5 juniper berries
1 tsp black peppercorns
1 tsp mustard seeds
12 young herring (matjes) fillets (about 2¹/₂ oz each)

Prep time: 20 minutes
Marinating time: 2 days
(in a cool place)

Per serving (8) approx.:
371 calories
30 g protein/15 g fat/18 g carbohydrates

1 Peel onions and slice, making rings. Heat vinegar, wine, sugar and the spices in a pot, and bring to a brief boil. Add onions, bring the liquid to a boil once more, turn off heat, and let it cool.

2 Meanwhile, rinse the herring fillets with cold running water. Pat them dry with paper towels, and cut into bite-sized pieces.

3 Take the onions out of the liquid with a skimmer. Alternating, put herring and onions into a high-sided earthenware or glass dish, and cover with the liquid.

4 Cover the dish with a lid or plastic foil. Allow the herring to stand in a cool place for 2 days. Served with potatoes boiled in the jacket. The preserved herring makes a complete meal for 6 people. Served with pumpernickel, it makes a hearty, quick bite. Tastes good with a beer.

VARIATION

Try the recipe with 1¹/₂ cups red wine vinegar and ¹/₂ cup sherry vinegar.

TIP!

Frequently young herring fillets (matjes) are available vacuum-packed in oil. As they are very salty, it is best to pour water over them and let them stand, covered, in the refrigerator for a few hours to desalinate.

Tarragon Chicken Fillets

● Sophisticated
● Easy

Serves 4:

3 sprigs fresh tarragon
1 sprig lovage
2 shallots
1 clove garlic
4 tbs tarragon vinegar
1½ cups chicken or vegetable stock
½ cup dry white wine or stock
1 bay leaf
Salt to taste
White pepper to taste
4 chicken breast fillets (5 oz each)
2 tsp cornstarch
⅓ cup crème fraîche
1 tsp Dijon mustard

Prep time: 40 minutes

Per serving approx.: 309 calories
28 g protein/19 g fat/5 g
carbohydrates

1 Wash herbs. Peel shallots and dice coarsely. Peel garlic and slice. Bring vinegar, stock, and wine to boiling in a pot. Add bay leaf, shallots, garlic, lovage, and 2 sprigs of the tarragon. Season with salt and pepper. Simmer the liquid, uncovered, for 15 minutes.

2 Meanwhile, sprinkle the chicken fillets with salt and pepper. Sprinkle with 1 tsp of the cornstarch and gently rub it in. Pour the liquid through a strainer into a saucepan, then heat it. Add the chicken breast fillets, and simmer, covered, at low heat for 5 minutes. Then turn the fillets, and simmer an additional 5 minutes.

3 Take the chicken from the liquid and keep it warm. Whisk together the crème fraîche, the remaining cornstarch, mustard, and 4 tbs of the cooking liquid. Stir the crème fraîche mixture into the liquid. Simmer the sauce, uncovered, for 2 minutes. Cut the remaining tarragon fine, and mix into the sauce.

4 With an eggbeater, beat the sauce until slightly foamy. Garnish the chicken fillets with the tarragon sauce. Serve with rice.

VARIATION

Chicken Fillets with Chervil Sauce
Instead of tarragon vinegar, use parsley vinegar (see page 16), then, instead of cooking the 2 sprigs tarragon in the liquid, use 2 stalks parsley. Mix ½ bunch, washed, and finely chopped chervil into the sauce.

Leg of Veal in Wine Vinegar Sauce

● For guests
● Prepare ahead

Serves 4:

4 slices leg of veal (10½ oz each)
Salt to taste
Black pepper to taste
2 cloves garlic
4 sprigs fresh thyme
3 tbs olive oil
1 cup dry white wine (e.g. white Burgundy)
⅓ cup red wine vinegar
1 tsp balsamic vinegar
6 whole allspice
½ lb small shallots
3 tbs peanut oil
2 tbs cane sugar
1 bay leaf
¾ lb carrots
1 stalk leek
½ cup veal or chicken stock
1 bunch fresh Italian parsley

Prep time: 40 minutes
Cooking time: 1 hour 30 minutes

Per serving approx.: 391 calories
20 g protein/17 g fat/37 g
carbohydrates

1 Rub meat with salt and pepper. Peel garlic and dice fine. Strip thyme leaves off stems. Mix oil with garlic and thyme, and baste the meat with the herb oil. Mix wine and vinegar. Crush allspice in a mortar.

2 Preheat the oven to 400°F. Peel the shallots. Heat oil in an ovenproof skillet. Sear the meat on both sides. Briefly fry the shallots as well. Sprinkle with 1 tbs of sugar, season with allspice, and add the bay leaf. Add the vinegar mixture to the skillet.

3 Put the skillet in the oven. Braise meat and shallots, covered, for 1 hour. Peel carrots and slice. Trim leek, wash, and slice into rings. Place carrots and leek around the meat, sprinkle with the remaining sugar, and season with salt and pepper. Pour veal stock over meat and vegetables, and braise for an additional 30 minutes.

4 Wash parsley and chop fine. Serve the veal slices with the vegetables, and sprinkle with parsley. Ribbon noodles make a good side dish.

TIP!

The meat can be basted with the spice oil the day before. Cover, and refrigerate. Prepare shallots and vegetables shortly before use. While the veal leg is being braised in the oven, you have plenty of time to take care of hors d'oeuvres and a dessert!

In the photo above:
Tarragon Chicken Fillets
In the photo below:
Leg of Veal in Wine
Vinegar Sauce

Spicy Savory Olive Cake

- Sophisticated
- Prepare ahead

Makes 1 loaf (standard bread-loaf size):

2 onions
$1/4$ lb smoked ham
$2/3$ cup olive oil, divided
4 oz pimiento-stuffed green olives
$1^1/4$–$1^1/2$ lb flour
2–3 oz freshly grated Gruyère cheese
2 packets dry yeast
1 cup lukewarm milk
2 eggs
Oil for greasing the baking pan

Prep time: 45 minutes
Rising time: 30 minutes
Baking time: 35–40 minutes

Per serving (18 slices) approx.:
212 calories
7 g protein/8 g fat/28 g
carbohydrates

1 Peel onions and dice. Cut ham in fine strips. Heat 3 tbs of the olive oil. Sauté onions in oil for 3 minutes. Mix in ham strips, and allow to cool. Drain olives in a strainer. Grease a standard-size bread pan.

2 Mix flour, cheese, and dry yeast in a bowl. Add milk, eggs, and the remaining olive oil, and knead together with the kneading attachment of a mixer, adding more flour as necessary to make a dough that cleans the sides of the bowl. Add onion-ham mixture, and knead in by hand until dough is elastic (about 8 minutes).

3 Place one third of the dough into the baking pan. Spread half of the olives on top. Cover with an additional third of the dough. Spread the remaining olives on top, and cover with the remaining dough. Cover, and allow to rise at room temperature for 30 minutes. Preheat the oven to 400°F.

4 Bake the cake in the preheated oven for 35–40 minutes. Serve lukewarm or cold.

TIP!

Together with a salad, the olive cake makes a delicious snack. It's also good with a glass of red wine. The cake can be frozen for later use.

Mini Flat Cakes with Herb Oil

● For guests
● Easy

Makes 6 flat cakes:

For the dough:
½ cup nonfat quark
or farmer's cheese
1 cup flour
1½ level tsp
baking powder
4 tbs corn oil
1 pinch salt

For the topping:
½ can water-packed tuna
⅓ cup canned,
chopped tomatoes
2 tsp dried oregano
Salt to taste
Black pepper to taste
2 tbs grated Gouda cheese
3 tbs herb oil with oregano
or thyme (see page 34),
for basting
Grease for the
baking sheet

Prep time: 30 minutes
Resting time: 30 minutes
Baking time: 25 minutes

Per flat cake approx.: 277 calories
10 g protein/19 g fat/18 g
carbohydrates

1 Drain quark or farmer's cheese in a strainer, lined with a cloth. Squeeze liquid out of the cheese.

2 Mix flour and baking powder in a bowl. With the knead attachment of a mixer, knead it together with oil, quark, and salt to make a dough, adding a bit more water if dough is dry, until it cleans the sides of the bowl. Finish kneading the dough by hand. Cover, and allow to stand in a cool place for 30 minutes. Grease the baking sheet. Preheat oven to 350°F.

3 For the topping, drain tuna in a strainer. Crumble fish apart with a fork.

4 Shape the dough into a roll and cut into 6 pieces. Push each piece by hand into flat round cakes, and put them on the baking sheet. Spread tuna and tomatoes on the flat cakes. Season with oregano, salt, and pepper, and sprinkle with cheese.

5 Bake the flat cakes in the preheated oven for 25 minutes. After 10 minutes, baste with half of the herb oil. At the end of the baking time, baste with the remaining oil. Best served warm with an apéritif.

VARIATION

If you like it hot, dribble the flat cakes with Chili Oil (see page 34) instead of the Herb Oil. The flat cakes are especially good if you baste them with Porcini Mushroom Oil (see page 35).

Vinegar Fruits Sweet-Sour

● Specialty from Italy
● Takes a bit of time

**Makes 4 jars
(2 cups each):**

1 lb peaches
1 organic orange
1 organic lemon
$^1/_3$ cup raisins
$^1/_4$ lb dried apricots
$^1/_4$ lb pitted prunes
1 lb tart apples
1 lb firm pears
$^1/_4$ cup lemon juice
$1^2/_3$ cups white
wine vinegar
$1^2/_3$ cups dry white wine
$1^1/_3$ cups sugar
1 tsp whole cloves
1 tsp whole coriander
1 tsp white peppercorns
2 cinnamon sticks
8 whole cardamom
8 star anise
4 tbs mustard seeds

Prep time: 1 hour 15 minutes
Storing: 3 months
(in a cool place)

Per jar approx.: 766 calories
7 g protein/5 g fat/175 g
carbohydrates

1 Bring a large pot of water to boiling. Blanch the peaches for half of a minute. Drain and immediately immerse in cold water. Skin the peaches, cut in half and pit them, then quarter them.

2 Wash the orange and lemon, and rub dry with a kitchen towel. Slice citrus fruits crosswise, about $^1/_2$ inch thick, cut these slices in half.

3 Wash raisins, and drain in a colander or strainer. Cut the apricots and prunes in half.

4 Peel apples and pears, quarter them lengthwise, and remove the cores. Immediately drizzle with lemon juice, so that the fruit does not discolor.

5 Put vinegar, wine, sugar, cloves, coriander, peppercorns, cinnamon, cardamom, star anise, and mustard seeds in a large pot, and bring to boiling. Simmer everything, uncovered, for 5 minutes.

6 Put peaches, apples, pears, lemon, and orange into the liquid, and cook at a boil, uncovered, for 7 minutes. The fruits should be covered with liquid. Add dried fruits, and simmer 1 additional minute. Remove the pot from the stove, and let the fruit stand overnight in the liquid.

7 Drain fruits in a colander, saving the liquid, and bring the liquid to boil in a pot. Simmer it for 10 minutes, uncovered.

8 Meanwhile, loosely layer the fruits into the jars. Cover the fruits with the hot liquid. Immediately close the jars. Mustard fruits are an ideal, classic side dish for cooked meat, cold roast, and game. They are also delicious with fondue, cold puff pastries, or toast with cheese.

Successful preserving of fruits and vegetables

• The jars must be thoroughly cleaned and rinsed with hot water.

• Jars with twist-off lids are practical. Collect jelly jars, pickle jars, etc., ahead of time. The content size is on the label, or sometimes on the bottom of the jar. Special canning jars with rings and metal clasps also work well.

• When filling the jars, place them on a damp kitchen towel. That way the heat is conducted away, and they do not crack.

• Fill the jars as much as possible up to the very top and close them immediately.

TIPS!

Mustard fruits are a popular gift. Layered in tall, slender, attractive jars, they make an especially pretty gift. Make sure that the jars can be tightly closed. The mustard syrup can be used to season tomato sauces. It also rounds out the flavor of sauces for vegetable salads with carrots, fennel, or celery.

Pineapple in Raspberry Vinegar

● Sophisticated
● Exotic

**Makes 1 jar
(2²/₃ cups each):**

1 pineapple (about 2 lb)
1 tbs green preserved peppercorns
1 cup raspberry vinegar (homemade, see page 16–17 or store bought)
1 vanilla pod
¹/₄ cup sugar
4 cloves
1 pinch ground nutmeg
²/₃ cup freshly squeezed orange juice

Prep time: 30 minutes
Storing: 2 months

Per jar approx.: 502 calories
3 g protein/2 g fat/129 g carbohydrates

1 Cut off the pineapple top. Cut the fruit in quarters lengthwise. Remove the woody core. Cut the fruit from the shell, and cut lengthwise into pieces about ¹/₂ inch thick. Catch and reserve the fruit juice. Rinse green peppercorns with water in a sieve.

2 In a pot, bring vinegar, vanilla pod, sugar, cloves, peppercorns, and nutmeg to boiling. Add pineapple with its juice and the orange juice. Simmer fruit pieces, uncovered, for 10 minutes, stirring occasionally.

3 Add pineapple and the liquid into an appropriate, preheated jar, and close immediately. The pineapple pieces go well with Asian rice dishes, as well as lightly smoked pork loin. They also taste great with raclette. The vinegar liquid is a good addition to tender green salads.

VARIATION

Instead of raspberry vinegar use a Blossom Vinegar with rose petals (see page 17).

Papaya in Cane Sugar Vinegar

● Fast
● Sophisticated

**Makes 2 jars
(2²/₃ cups each):**

2 ripe papayas (about 2 lb)
2¹/₂ inch piece fresh ginger
1 organic orange
³/₄ cup sugar cane vinegar
1 cup sugar
2 cinnamon sticks
4 cloves
6 allspice corns

Prep time: 25 minutes
Storing time: 3 months

Per jar approx.: 645 calories
3 g protein/1 g fat/169 g carbohydrates

1 Peel papayas and remove the seeds. Coarsely dice the fruit. Peel ginger and slice fine. Wash orange with hot water, peel it thin, and cut the peel in strips.

2 Bring vinegar, ³/₄ cup water, sugar, ginger, orange peel, and spices to boiling. Cover, and simmer for 8 minutes.

3 Add papaya pieces, and quickly bring to a boil on high heat, then simmer, uncovered, at medium heat for 1 minute. Put papaya and liquid into jars, and close immediately. The papaya goes well as a side dish with exotic meat dishes, or as a fruity addition to a sophisticated green salad like with iceberg or radicchio.

VARIATION

Instead of cane sugar vinegar, use fruit vinegar, mixed with 1 tbs honey or Honey Vinegar (see page 14). Another possibility is the use of Orange Vinegar (see page 17). In that case, you can use the orange peel spiral from the orange vinegar, and forego using any additional orange peel.

Sweet Lime Dish

● Spicy
● Exotic

Makes 2 jars (2 cups each):

3 organic sweet limes
3 organic lemons
3 red chile peppers
2 tbs salt
1 Spanish onion
2 tbs soy oil
1 cup fruit vinegar
5 tbs Tequila,
at your discretion
1 bay leaf

Prep time: 1 hour
Marinating time: 5 hours
Storing time: 3 months

Per jar approx.: 319 calories
4 g protein/14 g fat/44 g carb

1 Wash fruits, dry, and cut in quarters lengthwise. Remove seeds from chile peppers, and cut in strips lengthwise. Mix fruits, chiles, salt, and allow to stand, covered, for 5 hours.

2 Peel onion, slice into rings. Heat oil, sauté onion in oil for 2 minutes. Add all ingredients and 5 tbs water. Cover, simmer for 30 minutes. Put fruits and the hot liquid into jars. Close at once. Goes well with a Mexican buffet, or as a side dish for fish.

In the photo from top to bottom: Pineapple in Raspberry Vinegar, Papaya in Sugar Cane Vinegar, Sweet Lime Dish.

Zucchini Chutney

● For storing
● Exotic

Makes 2 jars (1¹/₂ cups each):

2 lb small zucchini
6 cloves garlic
2 inch piece ginger root
6 whole coriander
1 tsp salt
1 tsp chili powder
1 tsp cumin
1 tsp Garam Masala (from an East Indian or Asian store)
1 cup cane sugar
¹/₂ cup malt or beer vinegar

Prep time: 1 hour
Storing time: 3 months

Per jar approx.: 495 calories
7 g protein/2 g fat/123 g carbohydrates

1 Wash zucchini and slice very fine. Peel garlic and press through garlic press. Peel ginger and grate coarsely. Crush coriander in a mortar.

2 Put zucchini, garlic, ginger, coriander, and all other ingredients into a pot, and heat. Simmer vegetables, uncovered, at a low temperature for 45 minutes, stirring occasionally. The chutney has to become somewhat thick.

3 Fill the finished chutney into preheated jars while hot, and close immediately. The chutney goes well with stir-fried meat and with Asian rice dishes.

TIP!

Chutney can also be frozen.

Pumpkin Chutney

● For storing
● Exotic

Makes 4 jars (1¹/₂ cups each):

3 lb pumpkin (or other winter squash)
³/₄ lb red onions
5 cloves garlic
¹/₃ cup sultanas (golden raisins)
1 tbs soy oil
1 tbs mustard seeds
2 bay leaves
2 star anise
1 tsp salt
1²/₃ cups fruit vinegar
1¹/₄ cups cane sugar
1 tbs lemon juice

Prep time: 1 hour 30 minutes
Storing time: 3 months

Per jar approx.: 430 calories
4 g protein/3 g fat/107 g carbohydrates

1 Peel pumpkin, cut in half, and remove the seeds. Cut pumpkin in about ¹/₂ inch cubes. Peel onions and dice. Peel garlic and dice fine. Wash sultanas.

2 Heat oil in a pan. Sauté mustard seeds and onions for 1 minute. Add pumpkin, sultanas, garlic, bay leaves, star anise, salt and vinegar, and mix well.

3 Bring mixture to a boil. Simmer, uncovered, for 45 minutes, stirring occasionally. Stir in sugar and lemon juice. Continue to simmer, uncovered, for an additional 15 minutes. Put chutney into jars, and close at once. Pumpkin chutney goes well with pork roast and rice dishes.

Plum Chutney with Mint

● For storing
● Spicy

**Makes 2 jars
(1¹/₂ cups each):**

1 lb plums
3 white onions
2 tart apples
2 red chile peppers
24 fresh mint leaves
²/₃ cup lemon vinegar (see page 13, 17)
1 cup sugar
¹/₂ tsp ground allspice
Salt to taste
Black pepper to taste

Prep time: 1 hour 30 minutes
Storing time: 3 months

Per jar approx.: 660 calories
5 g protein/2 g fat/166 g
carbohydrates

1 Wash plums, cut in half, pit, and slice. Peel onions and chop fine. Wash apples, peel, remove core, and dice fine. Wash chile peppers, cut in half lengthwise, remove seeds, and cut in strips. Wash mint and cut in strips.

2 Bring vinegar, and sugar to a boil in a pot. Stir in allspice, salt, pepper, chile peppers, and mint. Mix in plums, onions, and apples. Simmer, uncovered, at a low heat for 1 hour, stirring occasionally.

3 Put chutney into jars and close immediately. The chutney goes best with lamb dishes.

Tomato Yellow Pepper Chutney

● For storing
● Easy

**Makes 2 jars
(1¹/₂ cups each):**

2 beef tomatoes
2 yellow bell peppers
1 lb Spanish onions
3 dried apricots
1 tbs peanut oil
1 tsp cumin seeds
1 tsp fennel seeds
3 cloves garlic
Salt to taste
³/₄ cup cane sugar
4 tbs lemon juice
³/₄ cup honey vinegar

Prep time: 1 hour 15 minutes
Storing time: 2 months
(refrigerated)

Per jar approx.: 636 calories
7 g protein/5 g fat/155 g carb

1 Pour boiling water over tomatoes, skin them, remove the seeds, and dice fine. Wash bell peppers, cut in half, trim, and cut in strips. Peel onions and dice small. Cut apricots in strips.

2 Heat oil in a pan. Briefly sauté cumin and fennel seeds in the oil. Add bell peppers, tomatoes, onions, apricots, and garlic. Sauté everything for 2 minutes, then mix in salt and sugar.

3 Add lemon juice and vinegar. Cook the chutney, uncovered, at medium temperature for 45 minutes until rather thick, stirring occasionally. Put the hot chutney into jars and close immediately. It tastes good served with barbecued meat.

Credits

Published originally under the title Essig & Öl © 1997
Gräfe und Unzer Verlag GmbH, Munich
English translation for the U.S. market ©2001,
Silverback Books, Inc.

All rights reserved. No part of this book may be repro-
duced in any form without the written permission of
the publisher.

Project editor: Lisa M. Tooker
Food editor: Terri Pischoff Wuerthner, CCP
Editor: Christine Wehling
Reader: Bettina Bartz
Layout, typography and cover design: Heinz
Kraxenberger
Typesetting and production: BuchHaus Robert Gigler
GmbH and Patty Holden
Output: Helmut Giersberg
Photos: Odette Teubner, aigner impuls (p. 6,8),
Bildagentur J. Dziemballa (p.9,29,30),
Stockfood/CEPHAS, Mick Rock (p.11),
Informationsgemeinschaft Olivenöl (p.20,23,25),
Neumeister (p.22,24)
Reproduction: Fotolito Longo, I-Frangart

ISBN: 1-930603-21-5
Printed in Hong Kong through Global Interprint,
Santa Rosa, California.

Annette Heisch
Heisch was born and raised in the culinary town of
Baden, and thus she inherited the love for fine food
and drink. She worked for several years as a food editor
for various women's magazines. Since 1995 she has
worked as freelance journalist and cookbook author.

Odette Teubner
Teubner grew up among cameras, floodlights, and
experimental kitchens, receiving her training from her
father, the internationally-known food photographer,
Christian Teubner. After a brief excursion into the
field of fashion, she returned to food photography,
and has since had the rare fortune to combine
profession and hobby.